**This book is dedicated to today's children and teenagers –
and those yet to come:**

May you grow up free to eat, live and thrive with a happy,
healthy relationship with food, as diets become a thing of the
past and wellbeing comes before profit.

This book was written in the hope that one day, it won't be
needed at all.

PRAISE FOR THIS BOOK

Alicia and I first met many years ago during her professional training and I've always known her to be a dedicated, skilled and thoughtful practitioner. In Mind How your Kids Eat, Alicia offers a refreshingly intelligent, sensitive and solution-focused guide that addresses the problems around eating food with clarity, empathy and practical wisdom that only decades of therapeutic and educational experience can bring. I was also pleased to see the inclusion of often-overlooked topics such as food anxiety, ARFID and the sensory sensitivities commonly experienced by neurodivergent children. Alicia has created a truly invaluable guide – one that will no doubt become a trusted companion for families seeking a gentler, more psychologically-informed approach to food and eating.

Dr Tom Barber – Psychotherapist, Educator, Founder of Self-Help School

This book needs to be on the reading list for all those privileged with the health and wellbeing of children, not just parents and carers but all those involved in the primary health care of children. Alicia has expertly covered, with her usual kindness and wisdom, the multiplicity of factors involved in how children develop their relationship to food and their own bodies, alongside providing an accessible set of tools and insights aimed at ensuring that children can learn to nourish themselves with kindness and lead healthy and vibrant lives. Alicia, is on paper, as warm, kind and skilled as she is in person, this book has been a pleasure to read and I highly recommend it to all.

Helen Golstein – Wellbeing Specialist, MSc Applied Positive Psychology, BSc Health & Education, Cert.Ed

As a psychotherapist with extensive experience supporting adults with weight issues, emotional eating, disordered food relationships, I wholeheartedly recommend Mind How your Kids Eat to parents, educators and clinicians alike. Alicia's emphasis on early habit formation, emotional awareness and mindful language is not only well-evidenced but profoundly empowering for parents who want to avoid repeating generational patterns. A powerful tool for prevention, healing and lasting change.

Dr Sandra Westland (D.Prof), MA, Bed

Mind How your Kids Eat is a book that is reassuring and insightful. Alicia integrates professional knowledge with honest storytelling in a way that makes you feel understood, not judged. With its' balance of behavioural strategies and deep emotional understanding, this book deserves to play a part in every family's journey towards healing their relationship with food.

Dr Joachim Lee PBM, Principal Psychotherapist, Author of Brain-Switch 2.0

This is a wise and timely book that shows how early emotional patterns and subconscious beliefs quietly shape eating habits for life – and what we can do to gently shift them. A highly recommended read for all parents and professionals working with children.

Jason Pegler – CEO Chipmunka – The Mental Health Publisher

This book draws a powerful link between children's early emotional world, the subconscious, and their lifelong relationship with food. An essential guide for parents and professionals alike.

Louise Baker – Applied Neuroscience Behavioural Specialist, MSc Psychology & Neuroscience in Mental Health

ALSO BY ALICIA EATON

Stop Bedwetting in 7 Days – 2009, 2012, 2019
(Practical Inspiration Publishing)

First Aid for your Child's Mind – 2019
(Practical Inspiration Publishing)

Words that Work: How to Get Kids to Do Almost Anything – 2015
(Troubador Publishing)

Fix your Life with NLP – 2012
(Simon & Schuster)

Visit website: www.aliciaeaton.co.uk for further details of online
programmes and hypnosis downloads for adults and children.

Mind How Your Kids Eat

Alicia Eaton

Troubador Publishing Ltd
Unit E2 Airfield Business Park
Harrison Road, Market Harborough
Leicestershire LE16 7UL
Tel: 0116 279 2299
Email: books@troubador.co.uk
Web: www.troubador.co.uk

ISBN 978 1836285 366

British Library Cataloguing in Publication Data.
A catalogue record for this book is available from the British Library.

The manufacturer's authorised representative in the EU for product
safety is Authorised Rep Compliance Ltd, 71 Lower Baggot Street,
Dublin D02 P593 Ireland (www.arccompliance.com).

Printed and bound in Great Britain by 4edge Limited
Typeset in 12pt Minion Pro by Troubador Publishing Ltd, Leicester, UK

CONTENTS

INTRODUCTION

I first wrote this book in 2008 – and honestly, I thought it would never see the light of day. Despite having the support of a well-respected literary agent and direct access to some of the top publishers in London, it was rejected.

Six times.

Each one said no – for reasons that, in hindsight, seem short-sighted. Perhaps I was just ahead of my time.

By then, I'd already spent some years working as a Harley Street Psychotherapist and Clinical Hypnotherapist, and I'd trained with Paul McKenna – recognised as one of the world's experts in the field of behaviour change – in NLP (Neuro-Linguistic Programming).

For over seven years I was an Assistant on his renowned Weight Loss Seminars – powerful, emotional days where hundreds of people would gather to unpack the real reasons behind their disordered eating. At that time, Paul understood, more than most, that weight problems are rarely about food – it's about psychology. And that diets, in most cases, simply don't work.

At the end of each seminar, during the Q&A, there would always be that one trembling voice asking: **'Please… how can I stop this from**

happening to my children? I don't want history to repeat itself.'
That question always landed in the room with impact – full of fear.

I'd had plenty of experience working with children – as a Montessori teacher running my own school and later, studying Developmental Psychology at the Anna Freud Centre in London. I'd also taken specialist childhood obesity training at the National Centre for Eating Disorders.

Not only did I understand the workings of a young child's mind, but I could see exactly how to create a programme of practical, empowering tools for parents – so they could indeed, help their children avoid growing up with weight problems and all the emotional eating issues that so often accompany them: food fussiness, anxiety, cravings, and sugar-dependence.

I knew I was best placed to write such a book – but the publishing world wasn't quite ready. One of them told me that as I wasn't a nutritionist or dietician, I wasn't qualified to write about eating.

But I wasn't writing a book about nutrition. I was writing a book about psychology – about the habits and behaviours that shape our relationship with food, many of which begin in childhood and last a lifetime.

At the time, there was still limited recognition of how this influences the way we eat. So instead, I turned my attention to other areas where parents were struggling in silence.

Over the years, I've written books on childhood bedwetting, anxiety, and behavioural change – all rooted in my work as a therapist and educator. These books have helped thousands of families all around the world, and each one taught me the same thing: when you offer parents calm, practical tools for difficult problems, you make a real difference.

And now, I'm ready to return to the subject I started with all those years ago.

Mind How Your Kids Eat is my latest parenting manual, designed to help families navigate children's eating habits: food anxiety, fussy eating, cravings for ultra-processed snacks and the risks of becoming overweight and even obese.

While many children today are being pulled into patterns of ultra-processed snacking, emotional eating, and rising weight gain, others – particularly those with ADHD, Autism Spectrum Disorder (ASD), or ARFID (Avoidant Restrictive Food Intake Disorder) – are struggling with the opposite: food-related anxiety, extreme selectivity, and sensory sensitivities that can make everyday eating feel like a battleground.

These challenges may look very different on the surface, but they all deserve the same compassionate, practical support. Using my decades of experience as a therapist specialising in changing habits and behaviour, my goal is to help parents break generational cycles – so today's children don't grow into tomorrow's adults needing to diet.

This book isn't about telling you what not to eat – it's about helping you understand that the mealtime habits you create now, will stay with your child for a lifetime – and showing you the small steps you can take to ensure they grow up with happier, healthier outcomes.

Isn't that what every child deserves?

Change doesn't always begin with big campaigns or sweeping policies. More often, it starts quietly – in the lunchboxes we pack, the snacks we offer, and the choices we make at the end of a busy day.

There's now mounting evidence to suggest that the age of six is a critical tipping point in a child's weight journey. At the 2025 European Congress on Obesity, Dutch researchers shared a study showing that children who are overweight at six are highly likely to carry that weight into their teens and beyond. In other words: if we want to change the outcome for our children, we need to start earlier than we think. Not with diets or restriction – but with simple habits, made at home, that gently support balance and health from the beginning.

In addition, recent research from *The Lancet* confirms just how urgent this work is becoming – not just for future generations, but for the young people already growing up in our broken food environment.

Generation Z – the teenagers and young adults of today – are now showing the highest levels of ultra-processed food consumption and fastest-rising rates of obesity, despite being part of a generation once celebrated for rejecting smoking and drinking. They're not addicted to cigarettes – it seems they're becoming addicted to snack foods.

This shift should alarm us – and motivate us. Because it means that today's children are not just at risk of repeating the patterns of the past. They're growing up in a food landscape that's even more extreme than anything we've seen before.

This doesn't mean we need to panic – but it does mean we need to look much more closely at childhood. Because the habits we form in those first few years are often the ones that stick. And the good news is, when we gently shift routines and reshape how children relate to food in their early years, we're not just changing what they eat today – we're helping them to avoid so many health issues later in life.

If we truly want to raise a generation of children who feel good in their bodies and confident around food – free from the trap of emotional eating, restrictive diets, or poor health – then we need to work together. Schools, retailers, food manufacturers, and governments all have a part to play in creating a healthier, kinder environment. One that puts children's wellbeing above profit and makes the right choice the easy one.

This book is written with parents in mind – but the message is for everyone. Because when each of us takes small, steady steps, real change becomes possible. We can protect our children from a lifetime of struggle and give them something far more valuable: a calm, balanced relationship with food – and with themselves.

And that change? It can begin right now – with you.

If We Tolerate This, Will Our Children Be Next?

What Are We Really Feeding Our Children?

When I was out shopping with my 11-year old daughter one day, she asked me a question that stopped me in my tracks: *'Mummy, how old do you have to be to go on a diet?'*

I gave her a vague answer – that you could diet at any age – but she persisted. *'Yes, but when do you start?'*

To her, dieting was simply another milestone – like moving up a level in the Girl Guides or Scouts. She assumed it was something every woman did eventually.

When I asked why, she pointed to the rows of magazines and books around us in the shop. *'There are so many books about diets. It's everywhere. I just thought it's something all grown-ups have to do'.*

And in that moment, I realised she was right. She had absorbed an unspoken but powerful message – one that many children grow up with, often unnoticed.

Children are born with the most extraordinary ability to learn and adapt. Their minds are particularly absorbent in the first six years of life as their brains operate at lower frequencies – the same ones hypnotherapists use to access the subconscious.

This means that children are in a highly programmable state. They take in everything – not just what we tell them, but what we do, how we react, what we avoid, what we fear.

They notice:

- When we skip meals and call it 'being good'
- When we grimace in front of the mirror
- When we joke about being 'naughty' for eating cake
- When we reward them with food for good behaviour
- When we comfort them with sweets after a disappointment

Children aren't born worrying about their weight. These beliefs are absorbed – from adults, from media, from society. Where once it was magazines, now it's social media: TikTok, Instagram, YouTube. They watch influencers' 'what I eat in a day' videos, see body transformations, and hear language like 'I was good today' because someone skipped a dessert.

Our children are growing up in a world that measures worth in body size and shape, not character. We don't mean to send harmful messages but, these moments really do matter because our relationship with food and eating begins in childhood.

If we keep sending out the message that eating is challenging, being overweight is inevitable, that weight loss medications are the norm, we can't be too surprised if it all comes true.

Let's Make This the Last Generation That Struggles

We're entering a new era. Powerful medications like Ozempic, Wegovy and Mounjaro are changing the landscape of weight management for adults. And for many, they're genuinely life-changing – helping people take back control of habits that once felt unbreakable.

These medications can serve a purpose – especially for adults who feel trapped in long-standing unhelpful patterns of eating and are struggling with serious health conditions. If taking them helps someone regain control, reduce health risks, and model more balanced behaviours for their child – then that's a step forward.

But let's be clear: medication should not be the legacy we want to pass on. If we can help adults break the cycle now – if they can find their own reset, understand their habits, shift their thinking – then perhaps we really can prevent the next generation from needing the same pharmaceutical solutions.

Let's not pass the problem down. Let's pass down the learning.

We've been supersized – without realising it.

One of the quietest shifts in modern eating habits hasn't been the food itself – it's the portion sizes. Without most of us even realising it, the average meal has grown… and grown… and grown.

There was a time when a cup of coffee was, quite literally, a cup – holding no more than 150ml. Today, a 'medium' takeaway coffee often exceeds 350ml, with large or 'venti' options tipping 500ml or more. And it's not just the size that's changed. What used to be a simple black coffee or a splash of milk has turned into a dessert in disguise – loaded with syrup, whipped cream, sprinkles, and marshmallows.

Think about pizza. Not long ago, one pizza fed a family – adults might have two slices, children one. Now, individual pizzas are standard. The idea of sharing feels quaint – even inconvenient.

Or take roast chicken. A single bird would once feed a family of five, carved into modest portions, perhaps with leftovers for sandwiches the next day. Now? It's not unusual to be served half a chicken on your plate at a casual dining chain, along with chips, bread, and sauces – and still feel prompted to order dessert.

And here's the thing: children are growing up thinking this is the baseline. That this is what coffee looks like. That it's usual to finish a large meal alone, or that snacks are supposed to be double-sized. The more we see it, the more we accept it. Our internal portion radar becomes distorted.

But this book isn't about telling you what not to eat – it's about helping you see what's really going on around you. Because once we understand that, we can begin to make confident, lasting changes.

Why Food Is Always Emotional

From the very beginning of life, food is never just food. Picture a newborn baby, nestled into their mother's arms, gently feeding. What they're receiving in that moment isn't just milk – it's warmth, closeness, skin-to-skin contact and a feeling of security.

These early feeding experiences become some of the very first ways a child learns to feel calm, safe and connected to another human being.

In that moment, eating is emotional. And that emotional imprint forms a blueprint that stays with us – quietly shaping our relationship with food for the rest of our lives.

So it's no wonder that children turn to food for comfort, reward, or reassurance. Or that we, as adults, reach for snacks when we're tired or stressed. To pretend that eating is simply about nutrition – about fat vs. sugar, or calories in/calories out – is to miss something essential. Because food has always meant more than that.

Ultra-processed foods – packed with hidden sugars, artificial flavours, and just the right crunch – have been carefully designed to trigger those same comforting feelings we once got from a loving embrace and a full tummy. They're not just tasty. They're engineered to make us feel better. That's why they're so hard to resist – and why so many children today reach for them automatically, even when they're not truly hungry.

So if we want to shift our children's relationship with food, we need to go deeper than rules and recipes. We need to understand what food means to them emotionally – and help them find other ways to meet those same needs.

In the Therapy Room

However, our challenges with food and eating, extend beyond eating too much and too many of the wrong foods. The children and young adults I meet in my therapy room often come to me because they're fussy eaters or afraid of trying new foods. But the problems are usually far more complicated – they come carrying quiet, invisible burdens – guilt, fear, overwhelm, or the belief that something inside them is wrong or broken.

What I've learned, time and again, is that food is often just the surface. Beneath it lies something else: a moment of emotional pain that was never fully understood, a fear that wasn't given the chance to be heard, or a sense of shame that quietly grew in the silence.

Inside the therapy room, we don't force change. We simply pause long enough to listen – really listen. And in that space, healing begins. Not because of any magic words or techniques, but because the child or young adult in front of me finally feels safe enough to let go.

I've shared some stories from my therapy room throughout this book, not to impress, but to reassure – to remind parents that even the most tangled habits can unravel, with time, patience, and compassion. And sometimes, all it takes is one moment. One suggestion. One quiet shift in the way we see ourselves, or our children.

Sometimes, the change is subtle. A boy who sits through dinner without panic. A teenager who stops punishing herself with food. Two brothers who find comfort in each other's calm. These moments may not make headlines, but to the families involved, they are life-changing.

Because food is never just about food. It's about love, safety, identity, and belonging. And when we work from that place – the place beneath the plate – everything starts to change.

When the World Felt Dangerous

As life slowly began returning to normal after the pandemic, I started to notice something new. The children coming to see me weren't just fussy eaters or reluctant to try vegetables. They were anxious – deeply, physically anxious – about being sick.

They were avoiding food, gagging at mealtimes, and obsessively checking their bodies for signs of nausea. Many had experienced a single episode of vomiting – either themselves, or they'd witnessed someone else – and from that moment on, something changed. Eating no longer felt safe.

Before the pandemic, I might have seen one child like this every few months. But in the first few weeks after lockdown restrictions lifted, I saw eight.

Eight children. All with the same fear.

The messaging during those years was relentless. Germs are dangerous. People can make you ill. Wash your hands. Don't touch that. Be careful. Stay apart.

These messages were necessary, of course – but they didn't just land in the ears of adults. They landed in the minds and nervous systems of children, many of whom were still forming their sense of what it means to feel safe in the world. And when a child doesn't feel safe, one of the first places that fear shows up is at the dinner table.

When we feel under threat – real or imagined – the body's appetite shuts down. Swallowing becomes harder. Digestion slows. Even thinking about food can bring on a wave of panic. For many children, food had quietly become part of the threat. Or, at the very least, something to fearfully control.

This book isn't just about helping children eat better. It's also about helping them feel safer. About rebuilding trust in food, yes – but also in their bodies, their environments, and the grown-ups around them.

Because what we're really doing – meal by meal – is shaping how a child relates to the world.

2

The Hidden Power of Habits – and How They Shape Our Children

If you've ever felt in 'two minds' about something, it's because you really do have two minds – the conscious and the subconscious.

Your conscious mind can think about the past, present, and future – it's the part that reminds you to send that email, fill up the car with fuel, or buy a loaf of bread on the way home.

Because of that, many people assume the subconscious mind must be less important, as though it's simply a kind of filing cabinet for old memories. But nothing could be further from the truth.

In fact, the subconscious mind is far more powerful when it comes to determining how we think, act, and behave. It's the motor – the engine – that drives us.

Programmed from childhood by our environment and experiences, the subconscious stores all our habits and behaviours and acts as a personal autopilot.

Think back to when you first learned how to drive a car. At the beginning, you had to think very hard about everything: manoeuvring the car, steering safely, watching the road, checking the speed limit, perhaps changing gears and switching on the windscreen wipers – often all at once. That's a lot for the conscious mind to juggle. No wonder you felt exhausted after each lesson!

But over time, with practice, you relaxed into it. Before long, you could drive confidently – chatting to a friend, singing along to music, even eating a sandwich – all while still controlling the car.

That's because the repeated actions of driving were 'downloaded' into your subconscious mind. Once there, they freed up your conscious mind to focus on other things.

This clever system, designed to help us multitask and function efficiently, can also be our downfall. The subconscious mind isn't all that picky and choosy about which habits it downloads and stores, so we can end up with patterns of behaviour that don't always serve us well.

The subconscious mind doesn't judge habits as good or bad. It only cares whether something is familiar. And to the primitive part of our brain, familiar equals safe. Even if a habit is causing problems, the brain may cling to it – because predictability feels secure.

This is why real change often stirs up resistance. It's not just about doing something new; it's about letting go of something that feels safe and emotionally meaningful.

Imagine asking someone to start supporting a different football team from the one they've cheered for all their life. Even if they really wanted to make the change, it would still feel odd and uncomfortable to swear allegiance to a former rival and wear different colours. There's a loyalty and a deep emotional bond wrapped around that habit – and it's exactly the same when it comes to other areas of life, like food and family traditions.

Habits that become deeply ingrained in childhood tend to stick and once they're established as part of our autopilot system, they can be hard to erase.

Children Are Programmed Faster – and More Deeply

And as I've mentioned, children's brains operate at a lower frequency than adults. In their early years, they spend more time in Theta and Delta brainwave states – the same hypnotic states that therapists use to access the subconscious mind.

What this means is that everything in a child's environment is being absorbed – not just language and manners, but beliefs, fears, behaviours, and emotional responses. They don't just hear our words – they internalise our attitudes.

Which means that if we, as adults, joke about our weight, skip meals, panic over calories, or equate food with guilt or control – we're teaching those same scripts to our children, even if we never say them out loud.

Our words matter – more than we realise. So let's make sure we're planting seeds of confidence, not confusion, at the dinner table and beyond.

3

What Our Childhood Teaches Us About How We Feed Our Children

Before we go any further, let me start by being honest with you. There's nothing worse than reading a book written by a so-called 'expert' whose family dinners look like something out of a lifestyle magazine – all home-cooked meals, no tantrums, and everyone thanking Mum for the broccoli. Am I right?

You find yourself wondering whether they really have any life experience – or any understanding at all, of the struggles you're facing.

'It's all right for them,' you think. And you wouldn't be wrong.

So I'm going to be upfront with you. I don't particularly enjoy cooking or spending hours in the kitchen. I don't collect recipe books, and I've never been a fan of TV baking shows. Yes, I cooked, fed, and raised three children – so I can do it, but I don't do it for fun.

That's why this book won't be offering you complicated nutritional advice or elaborate lunchbox ideas – and certainly not asking you to get up at 5am to cut star shapes into your cucumbers. That's not what matters most. What really makes the difference over time is the daily rhythm – the habits, routines, and unspoken messages that shape how children grow up feeling about food.

Our Childhood Mealtimes Leave Deep Imprints

I suppose one reason I've never been especially enthusiastic about cooking is because, truth be told, my own childhood mealtimes weren't always the most relaxed affair.

I was born in London, but my parents were both from Poland. While my friends tucked into bowls of Angel Delight – a sweet, mousse-like popular dessert – we were eating roast veal and sauerkraut. I was acutely aware that we were different – and when you're a child, different doesn't always feel good.

My father's childhood had been, shall we say, privileged. His family owned a large hotel on one of the main streets in Warsaw, complete with waiters, starched linen tablecloths, fine china plates, crystal glasses – and a five-piece band playing in the background during meals.

Our modest family dinners at home, understandably, never quite matched those memories – and my father's quiet disappointment often hung in the air.

In later years, as our family grew larger, he was at his happiest when there were 20 or so people sitting round the table – something that happened regularly. He craved large gatherings. Just opposite his seat was a sideboard groaning under the weight of extravagant fruit displays he'd arranged: huge bunches of grapes and pineapples stacked in shiny, oversized crystal bowls, replicating his childhood days in the hotel.

To add to the tension, my parents were highly competitive. It wasn't unusual for my mother to place a roast chicken on the table at the exact same moment my father brought in his roast pork – and we children were then asked to judge which dish was better. Trust me, there are no winners in games like that – and the audience doesn't much enjoy it either.

So, while there was always plenty of well-cooked food in our house, my memories of mealtimes weren't always fond ones. It's hardly surprising, then, that I grew up preferring to spend less time in the kitchen, than out of it.

Raising My Own Family: A Different Kind of Focus

When it came time to raise my own family, life was no less challenging. In my earlier book *'Words That Work: How to Get Kids to Do Almost Anything'*, I described how I was running my own Montessori school, navigating a divorce, and raising three children alone in a large, Edwardian house in need of constant repair.

One of my children was the fussiest eater on the planet. (You thought that child was yours? Believe me, we could compare notes.) Trying to win him over with carefully curated 'child-friendly' recipes from parenting books was an exercise in futility. I had as much chance of flying to the moon as I did of getting him to nibble on couscous and courgette bake. He was strictly a fish-fingers-only boy. You can read more about the struggles I had with him, in the chapter on fussy eating.

Another of my children could demolish a week's worth of sugary snacks in five minutes flat – which led me, in desperation, to hang a string of Swiss cowbells across the larder door as an early-warning system that it was being opened!

In those days, survival was the goal. Healthy meals were important, yes, but I didn't have the energy to become obsessed. What mattered most was that my children grew up happy, balanced, doing well at school – and that we enjoyed each other's company.

Did they eat chicken nuggets and fish fingers? Absolutely. As a single parent of three, outnumbered every day, I had to pick my battles. There was no point wasting precious energy trying to persuade small children to develop 'sophisticated palates'. Some things you simply have to let go. And looking back, I can see now: while the food may not have been perfect, the habits were good.

The Importance of How We Eat

However simple our meals were, they were always eaten properly: Served from the Aga, we sat at the table, with knives and forks, often with some classical music playing softly in the background.

It never occurred to any of us that mealtimes might happen slumped on the sofa, in front of the TV, pizza box in hand. It just wasn't the way we did things. Perhaps, in the end, a little of my father's formality had rubbed off on me.

Does this matter?

I believe it does. Because the way we do things – the tone, the timing, the togetherness – becomes part of a child's emotional script. What we eat can change. But how we eat? That sticks.

A Day in the Life of a Montessori School

I first began my career of working with children as a Montessori teacher and I was Principal of my own school for five years.

One of the things that always surprised prospective parents on viewing days was how we handled break time and snacks. In most traditional early years settings, break happens at a fixed time – usually around 10.30am. But Montessori philosophy encourages us to give children freedom and responsibility to make their own choices.

So, in my school, we offered a selection of chopped fruit and milk throughout the whole morning, and the children chose *when* they wanted to eat. To me, this made perfect sense.

Some children are up early and might have breakfast at 6.30am. Others could be seen finishing theirs as their parent's car pulled into the car park around 9.15am. Imposing a rigid schedule on such young children means some will go hungry, while others end up eating when they're not really hungry at all.

It makes you wonder: how many school-age children are eating because they're told to – and not because they actually need to?

Children are born with an in-built hunger mechanism. Just think of a newborn baby who cries when it's time to feed. Somewhere along the way, we stop trusting that signal – and start overriding it with adult-led rules. Sometimes we need to remind ourselves that children often know best when it comes to their own bodies.

Another thing that occasionally surprised parents was that the children served themselves – deciding whether they wanted a large or small portion. Because this was just part of everyday life, there was no sense of novelty. The children behaved responsibly, made good decisions, and – crucially – learned to listen to their own hunger cues.

We had just three chairs at the break table, so not everyone could eat at once. The children had to think about when to go, how long to stay, and whether to invite a friend to join them. There was a sense of gentle independence in all of it.

The break table was set with a proper tablecloth and a small vase of flowers. I bought small espresso cups and matching bowls made of real china – not plastic. Some people questioned the choice: wouldn't they break? But children notice when adults drink from nice crockery and hand them plastic. It sends a clear message – one that says: 'You're not trusted.'

And yet, over five years of running that school, we didn't have a single breakage. Everything stayed intact.

We even set up a small washing-up station. After eating, the children would rinse their own cups and bowls. Sometimes drinks were spilled, but they knew what to do: clear the table, fetch a clean tablecloth, and set it all up again. Then they'd wash the dirty one and peg it up to dry.

No one saw it as a chore or a punishment. It was just part of daily life. Sure, it would have been easier to have had a wipe-clean tablecloth – or not to have had one at all, but that wasn't the point. The point of having the cloth was to help the children think about what they were doing, concentrate and notice small details. And it worked.

Childhood mealtimes shape a lifetime of eating

So, what can we take from all of this?

I've shared some personal stories – from my own childhood, from raising my three children, and from my time running a Montessori school – not because they were perfect, but because they were real. And real life, as you know, is often messy and unpredictable. But within that messiness, certain patterns always emerge.

And over the past 20 years, in my work as a therapist, I've seen those patterns surface again and again. Every single client who's come to me for help with weight loss or eating struggles has had a story – a memory from childhood that left a mark.

Often, it's not about *what* they were eating, but how they were made to feel. A comment, a family routine, a rule about finishing everything on the plate, – these early experiences imprint themselves deeply, and they continue to shape how we relate to food, long into adulthood.

If we look closely, we can learn a lot from the way our own habits were formed – especially the ones that began at our childhood dinner tables. Because the way we're fed in the early years doesn't just fill our tummies – it leaves an emotional imprint. It quietly shapes the way we view food, family, and ourselves.

Let's reflect on this:

1. Children Learn What They Live
If you grew up with mealtimes that felt relaxed and happy, you'll probably find yourself naturally recreating that with your own children. But if mealtimes were stressful, rushed, or full of tension, some of that may have quietly travelled with you into adulthood.

Think back for a moment:
Were you praised for finishing everything on your plate?
Was food used as a reward or withheld as a punishment?

2. Family Traditions Shape Us Too

Food is rarely just food. It's culture. It's comfort. It's belonging. Whether you grew up with hearty Sunday roasts, spicy curries, plates of pasta, or supermarket-ready meals – those traditions shaped your ideas about what eating 'should' look like. But traditions can evolve. And sometimes they need to.

It's always worth asking yourself:
Are the old ways still serving my family now?
Or is there room for something new?

3. Food and Feelings Get Tied Together

Food is emotional – it always has been and always will be. If you were comforted with sweets when you were sad, or made to feel guilty about leaving food behind, you might find echoes of those experiences in how you parent now.

The goal isn't to strip food of emotion altogether. Food is about connection and joy. Keep love and care are at the centre of the experience – not guilt, pressure, or fear.

Teaching your child to listen to their own body – to know when they're full, to trust their hunger cues – is one of the greatest gifts you can give.

4. You Get to Break the Cycle – If You Want To

One of the loveliest things about parenting is that it gives us a chance to do things differently. It's not about blame. It's not about getting everything perfect. It's about saying: '*This worked for me, I'll keep it*' – and '*This didn't feel so good, maybe I'll try something else.*'

Ask yourself:

What did you love about the way you were fed as a child?

What would you like to do differently now?

When you put your energy into connection, kindness, and good habits, you build something far more powerful than any one meal: You build a foundation your child will carry with them for life.

Your Family Mealtimes

Take a few moments to sit down and answer these questions. You may learn something new today.

1. **How would you describe mealtimes in your childhood home?**
   - ☐ A happy, relaxed time
   - ☐ A stressful experience
   - ☐ Just something to get through
   - ☐ Other (please describe)

2. **What did you love most about mealtimes as a child?**

3. **What did you dislike about mealtimes as a child?**

4. **Were you expected to finish everything on your plate?**
   - ☐ Always
   - ☐ Sometimes
   - ☐ Rarely/Never

5. **How were treats and sweets handled in your home?**
   - ☐ Freely available
   - ☐ Given in moderation
   - ☐ Restricted/only for special occasions
   - ☐ Used as a reward or punishment

6. **What messages did you receive about food and eating from your parents or caregivers? (e.g., 'Eat everything because there are starving children in the world' or 'Food is fuel, not for fun')**

7. **Was there a structured mealtime routine, or was it more relaxed?**
   □ We ate together at the table every night
   □ It varied, but we often ate together
   □ Everyone ate separately, whenever they wanted
   □ Other (please describe)

8. **Were there frequent arguments or tensions around food and eating?**
   □ Yes, often
   □ Occasionally
   □ No, not really

9. **Were you an only child, or did you have siblings? How did that affect mealtimes?**
   □ I was an only child – it sometimes felt lonely
   □ I was an only child – I enjoyed the peaceful meals
   □ I had siblings – mealtimes felt competitive/a 'bun fight'
   □ I had siblings – mealtimes were noisy, but friendly and fun

10. **Looking back, do you feel your parents' approach to food was:**
   □ Too strict
   □ Too relaxed
   □ Balanced
   □ Other (please describe)

11. **Do you think your childhood food experiences have influenced the way you feed your own children? If so, how?**

12. **Are you a good role model for your child's eating habits?**

Now that you've taken a moment to reflect on how you were fed as a child, let's bring the focus to the present – to your own eating habits today.

The questions below aren't here to judge or criticise. They're simply an opportunity to pause and notice how your current habits might be shaping your child's relationship with food. Sometimes even the smallest behaviours – eating on the go, skipping meals, or labelling foods as 'bad' – can send powerful messages that stick.

This is about awareness, not perfection. You don't need to overhaul everything – just begin to spot the habits that might be worth reshaping, for your sake and theirs.

1. **Do you eat meals at the table, or do you often eat while doing other things (e.g., watching TV, working, scrolling on your phone)?**

2. **How often do you eat standing up, straight from the fridge or pantry?**
   □ Never
   □ Occasionally
   □ Frequently

3. **Do you eat in the car while driving or commuting?**

4. Does your phone, laptop, or workspace have crumbs, coffee stains, or sticky marks from eating while working?

5. Do you encourage family mealtimes, or does everyone eat separately?

6. Do you talk about food in a positive way, or do you often comment on diets, weight, or feeling guilty about eating certain foods?

7. Do you take the time to enjoy and appreciate food, or is eating often rushed and mindless?

8. How often do you sit down and eat with your child without distractions?
   ☐ Every day
   ☐ A few times a week
   ☐ Rarely

9. Do you model a balanced approach to food, eating a variety of foods without labeling them as 'good' or 'bad'?

10. Do you listen to your own hunger and fullness cues, or do you eat out of habit, stress, or boredom?

11. Do you drink enough water, or is your main source of fluids coffee, tea, or sugary drinks?

12. Would you want your child to develop the same eating habits that you currently have?

You've just taken an important first step – bringing awareness to the patterns that may have been shaping your family's relationship with food without you even realising it.

Remember, this isn't about blame or guilt. It's about understanding.

We all bring our own histories to the table – quite literally – and the more you understand where those habits come from, the more choice and freedom you have in how you move forward.

4

IT'S THE LITTLE THINGS THAT COUNT

Helping your child build a healthy relationship with food isn't about big, dramatic actions. It's not about sudden diets, strict rules, or sweeping changes. It's about small choices, made consistently, over time. It's about patience, trust, and understanding the way habits quietly shape a life.

In this chapter, I'm going to show you why steady, gentle changes win out over quick fixes – and how two simple but powerful ideas from psychology can guide the way you think about your child's eating habits, day by day.

The Surprising Power of Tiny Changes

There's a powerful idea I often share with my clients: it's the small things we do each day that create the biggest impact over time.
Darren Hardy sums this up so well in his book *The Compound Effect*: whether it's putting an extra sugar in your tea each morning or going for a short walk each evening, the long-term outcome of those small actions can be extraordinary. It's not about making one big, dramatic change – it's about the slow, steady build of consistent choices.

This applies just as much to our children's eating habits. A few extra snacks each week, oversized portions at dinner, or sweet treats becoming part of the daily routine – these things may feel harmless in the moment, but over the months and years, they quietly accumulate. And the result can be significant weight gain, low energy, or poor eating habits that follow a child into adulthood.

But the good news is, the reverse is also true.

Small, simple adjustments – like reducing portion sizes slightly, cutting out a daily sugary snack, or adding in a little more movement – will also compound. And over time, these positive habits gently steer your child towards a much healthier future.

It's important to say here: children should not be put on diets. That's not the answer. Restriction and guilt have no place at the family table. What works is a calm, measured approach – making thoughtful tweaks, encouraging better choices, and trusting the process.

If your child is currently carrying extra weight, there's no need to panic. Nature is on your side. Children grow. And when sensible changes are made to eating patterns and activity levels, their natural growth spurts will do a lot of the heavy lifting. As they get taller – and as long as eating habits remain balanced – they'll often slim down gradually without any pressure or stress.

This is a long-term project. You have around 15 years to help shape your child's relationship with food, their body, and their health. So take the pressure off. What matters most is consistency, not perfection.

Everything compounds – both the helpful and the unhelpful. Your job is simply to keep nudging things in the right direction.

Bit by bit, meal by meal, you're building the foundation for your child's lifelong wellbeing. And that's the real win.

A Penny That Turns Into Millions – And Why It Matters

One of the most powerful illustrations Darren Hardy shares in his book is what he calls the 'Magic Penny' exercise – a simple yet unforgettable metaphor for the power of compounding choices.

Imagine being given a choice:

Would you rather have £3 million in cash right now – or just one single penny that doubles in value every day for 31 days?

Most people would instinctively choose the £3 million. It seems like the obvious win. But if you chose the penny and waited patiently while it doubled – 2p on Day 2, 4p on Day 3, 8p on Day 4 – something extraordinary would happen.

By Day 10, you'd still have only just over £5.

And progress would continue to feel a little slow for a while longer.

By Day 20, you'd have accumulated a little under £5,500 – still a long, long way behind had you opted to take the millions.

By Day 25, even though the compounding effect is doing its' job, you'll still be behind, with just £176,000.

You'll have to wait till Day 29, to really start seeing results. On this day your one single penny will have grown to more than £2.5 million.

So the month is nearly over, and you're doing well – but you've still missed out.

But wait. This is where the magic begins.

On Day 30, you'll have over £5 million.

And by Day 31 – astonishingly: more than £10 million.

Now who's the loser?

That's the power of compound growth. It starts small, often feeling slow or invisible – but then momentum kicks in, and the results become staggering.

The same principle applies when you begin to shift your child's eating habits. The first few tweaks – new routines at mealtimes, swapping a snack, slightly reducing portion sizes, introducing one new vegetable a week, – may seem like they're not making a dent. But those small actions are quietly building up. And just like the magic penny, their effect compounds over time.

This is a long-term project. So don't rush. Don't over-correct. Just keep nudging gently in the right direction.

Small, positive choices – made consistently – will always beat big, dramatic changes that don't last.

If I were starting again with raising a family, here's the kind of framework I'd want to have in place – something simple, steady, and clear, to guide the daily rhythm of food and family life.

Take Small Steps – but make them good ones:

1. Stick to Consistent Mealtime Windows

While life doesn't always allow for strict schedules, having a general window for dinner each evening (say, between 5:30 and 6:00pm) gives your child's body and brain a rhythm to rely on. When meals happen at roughly the same time each day, appetite and mood tend to stabilize too. You might notice fewer tantrums, less resistance, and even better sleep patterns.

2. Eat All Meals at the Table

There's something powerful about sitting down at a table to eat – it sends a subtle but important message to children: this matters. It doesn't have to be a formal event, and it certainly doesn't need to be fancy, but leaving the sofa behind and switching off the television can help re-establish the idea that mealtimes deserve their own space. When you consistently eat at the table, food becomes a shared activity rather than a background to something else.

If you don't have a dining table then consider how else you could create a similar space – eg. placing a wipe-clean tablecloth on the floor with everyone sitting on cushions will help to frame your meal and anchor everyone down in one place. A picnic blanket in the garden or local park is another way of doing this.

3. Make a 'meal of a meal'

Children often arrive at the table still buzzing with energy or overstimulated from screens and activity. Shifting into mealtime mode takes a little help, and that's where a calming pre-dinner routine can work wonders. This might be as simple as turning down the lights, putting on soft music, or lighting a candle.

These small sensory signals help everyone – adults included – transition into a more relaxed state. Over time, the brain begins to associate these cues with slowing down, connecting, and eating calmly.

Add cloth napkins, put out a small vase of flowers, water jug with glasses, plates and cutlery before the meal begins. These tiny rituals signal to your brain (and your child's) that something meaningful is happening here. They help meals feel like events, rather than chores, and over time, children begin to mirror the respect and intention you bring to the table.

4. Create Digital-Free Mealtimes

Phones and tablets quietly disconnect us from what's really happening in the moment: the food on our plate and the people around us. When we remove digital distractions, we create space for attention, awareness, and eventually, connection. It might feel strange at first, but over time, this one change can transform the atmosphere at your table in ways that go far beyond food.

5. Stop Multi-tasking While Eating

It's tempting to use mealtimes to tick things off the to-do list – packing tomorrow's lunch, sorting the mail, or replying to that one last email. But when you multi-task, the meal loses its power to ground and connect. Instead, try treating mealtimes as their own little pause in the day, a moment of presence. You might be surprised how much calmer the atmosphere becomes when everyone – including you – can simply sit, eat, and be there together.

6. Put a Simple Meal Plan on Display

A meal plan doesn't have to be complicated or rigid. Even just jotting down three or four dinners for the week and sticking them on the fridge gives you a sense of structure to lean on. When the question 'What's for dinner?' is already answered, the stress of decision-making disappears, and you're far less likely to default to last-minute, less healthy options. Seeing the plan also helps children feel more secure – they know what to expect, and routine gives them the confidence to try new things.

7. Clear Visual Clutter from the Kitchen

Our surroundings influence our choices more than we think. When counters are cluttered and junk food is visible, it becomes harder to make intentional decisions – especially at the end of a long day. By clearing away packets of crisps, half-open biscuit tins, and the overflow of recycling, you create a calmer space that invites better choices. Even a simple fruit bowl or a clean, empty surface can change the way you feel about cooking and eating. A tidy kitchen often leads to a clearer mind – and that's a gift during the pre-dinner rush.

8. Tidy the Fridge and Pantry Weekly

You don't need to Marie Kondo the entire kitchen, but a five-minute tidy once a week can make a big difference. Throw out expired condiments, take note of what's left over, and reorganize the shelves just enough so you can see what you've got. This isn't just about cleanliness – it's about clarity. When your food storage areas feel manageable and inviting, you're more likely to want to cook and eat at home.

9. Delete Food Delivery Apps and Unsubscribe from Their Emails

Food delivery companies are clever. They know that 5pm is when your energy is low, your stress is high, and your patience is running on fumes. That's when the tempting notifications appear – '20% off tonight only!' – and suddenly, the plan to cook goes out the window. By simply removing these apps from your phone and unsubscribing from their mailing lists, you remove a powerful trigger that's designed to catch you at your weakest moment. It's a small action, but it gives you back a sense of control at the exact time you need it most.

These changes may seem small – almost too small to matter. But that's exactly where their power lies. When you create a home environment that supports calm, connected meals, you're not just tidying the kitchen or switching off the TV – you're shaping how your child thinks and feels about food.

These simple shifts lay the groundwork for something much bigger: habits that feel natural, sustainable, and nourishing for the whole family. And as with all lasting change, it begins with the smallest step.

5

Making Changes That Stick:
How to Build Habits That Last

By now, you've probably identified a few things you'd like to change. Perhaps it's your child's fussy eating, a constant battle over snacks, or a creeping reliance on takeaways.

It's natural (we're human beings, after all) to want to leap straight into action – to fix the problem and make things better as quickly as possible. But before we jump into the 'what' – the specific strategies for each issue – we need to pause and think about the *how*.

Because when it comes to changing your child's habits, how you go about it matters just as much as what you decide to change. It's the difference between a resolution that fizzles out in a week and a routine that transforms your family life for years to come.

The truth is, most change fails not because the idea is wrong – but because there's no real plan to support it. And in family life, a plan doesn't just mean lists and rules. It means preparing your environment, communicating clearly, involving your child, and building new habits gradually and consistently.

So, before we move on to individual challenges – let's get practical. Let's take a moment to build your **Parenting Toolkit**. These are the tools and frameworks that will support every change you make from this point forward.

This next section will help you map out where to begin, how to prioritise, and most importantly, how to make changes that actually stick.

You don't have to fill them out just yet – but I wanted you to read and understand them, first. That way, your mind will already be working on coming up with strategies for solving the problems you'll be reading about in the next few chapters.

STEP ONE: YOUR WISH LIST

To help you figure out where to begin, I've created something I call *The Wish List* – a simple but powerful tool to help you get clear on which habits or routines might need the most attention in your family right now.

I've created this Wish List with 25 spaces, but that does not mean you need to stop there – keep going if you want to. If you have a large family, it's possible your list will be twice as long.

Here are some examples of the areas you may want to focus on:
- Fussy eating habits
- Food anxieties and phobias
- Managing snack-related conflicts
- Reducing reliance on takeaways and convenience food
- Improving mealtime behaviour and routines
- Involving children in mealtime tasks (planning, prep, cooking, and clearing up)
- Weaning children off high-sugar foods

- Encouraging healthy drink choices
- Experimenting with new foods and increasing vegetable variety
- Organising the kitchen for better habits
- Establishing a simple meal plan
- Creating a calm, digital-free eating environment
- Supporting consistent bedtimes to improve appetite regulation

STEP TWO: GET SPECIFIC

If your problem area is something like 'fussy eating', then break it down. What, specifically, needs to change?

It might be:

- Lack of variety – eating the same few foods repeatedly
- Texture sensitivity – avoiding foods that are mushy, lumpy, or crunchy
- Anxiety around mealtimes – stress or meltdowns before or during meals
- Grazing all day – leading to disrupted hunger cues
- Strong food preferences – only bland or sweet foods tolerated
- Parental stress – tension in the room that your child picks up on

You don't need to finish this now. Keep reading and let the ideas simmer. This list may be something that you keep adding to and revisiting as time goes by. The goal is simply to raise your awareness so that, by the time you are ready to act, you'll know where to focus.

Wish List

1.	
2.	
3.	
4.	
5.	
6.	
7.	
8.	
9.	
10.	
11.	
12.	
13.	
14.	
15.	
16.	
17.	
18.	
19.	
20.	
21.	
22.	
23.	
24.	
25.	

STEP THREE: THE 80/20 RULE – WHY LESS IS MORE

Let me introduce you to a principle that will prove to be the most efficient way to start making changes to your family eating habits: the 80/20 rule.

Also known as the Pareto Principle, this idea comes from Italian economist Vilfredo Pareto who noticed that 80% of Italy's land was owned by 20% of the population. He even found that 80% of the peas in his garden came from just 20% of the pods! The same pattern applies across business, economics – and yes, even your home life.
Let's look at a few familiar examples:

Shoes in your wardrobe: You probably wear the same 20% of your shoes, 80% of the time. That's the ordinary everyday ones. The rest – the ones with sparkly heels, flip-flops, and party boots – barely see the light of day.

Your income: About 80% of your household budget likely goes on just 20% of your monthly bills. The remaining 20% of money is spread thinly across everything else.

Phone contacts: You talk to about only 20% of your contact list regularly. One or two of them probably take up most of your call time. Do you even remember who the remaining 80% are?

Family meals: Most families eat the same handful of meals over and over. A small rotation – maybe 20% of your recipe bank – accounts for 80% of your dinners. I'm going to guess, you're 'on repeat' when it comes to menu choices.

And so, we're going to apply the same principle to your Wish List too.
By the time you finish reading this book, you may end up having created a list of 20 or even 30 or more things you'd like to change about

your family's eating habits. I'm going to guess it may be significantly longer.

And so, you may end up with a very long to-do list which in all probability, won't make you feel terribly inspired at all. In fact, it will feel overwhelming – you won't know where to start – and so, like many of us, **you won't get started at all.**

The thing is, if we follow the Pareto Principle, we'll find that 20% of our efforts will yield 80% of our results. It's not just coincidence – it's a pattern of focus and efficiency.

And when it comes to habit change, that's why this rule matters.

Because not all habits carry equal weight. A small number of actions usually have a disproportionate impact – for better or worse. If you try to change *everything* at once, your energy gets scattered. But when you focus on the vital 20% – the few key behaviours that are really driving your family's food routines – you gain momentum. You see progress. And progress builds motivation.

This approach also prevents overwhelm. It shifts your mindset from 'I have to fix it all' to 'I just need to change a few key things.' That's empowering. That's sustainable. And that's how real transformation begins – one small but high-impact step at a time.

So here's what I want you to do:
- Count how many items are on your list.
- Divide that number by five. Eg. if you have 30 items, divide by five = 6.
- Now, choose that number of items from your list.
- Look for the ones that would make the biggest impact to a happy, healthy family life.

This is where you will start.

Let the rest go for now. You're not deleting them forever. You're simply focusing your time and energy on what will move the needle most.

And as you begin to tick those items off your list, you create space for the rest.

So, I recommend reading through the other chapters in this book first and as you're going through them, keep returning to this section to add items to your Wish List.

Make that list as long as you can because even if you're adding items that you're kind of in two minds about, they'll help you to gain clarity about which habits are the really important ones to focus on.

6

PUTTING IT INTO PRACTICE

Creating your Family Story around Food

The most important people affected by the changes you plan to make in your household are, of course, your family members: your children, your partner, and anyone else who shares your home.

That's why it's so important to include them in the process. When it comes to introducing new habits around food, one of the most effective ways to begin is by hosting a **'Family Meeting'**.

You can call it anything that feels right for you: Family Conference, Circle Time, Get-Together, Meet-Up, Session, or simply a Chat. What matters most is that it becomes a regular, relaxed opportunity for everyone to come together in a safe, supportive space. It should be a place where problems can be discussed, successes shared, and ideas explored – without judgment.

You might also include anyone who helps with childcare (like grandparents, a nanny, or a neighbour) in these conversations now and then, especially if they play a role in your child's eating routines.

Now, I know it might feel odd at first. Meetings? At home? But think about it: we have meetings at work, at school, with teachers, with friends over coffee – they're everywhere. And yet, when it comes to our own families, we rarely sit down with the same sense of intention and care.

When we skip that step, it's easy to fall into patterns of nagging, reacting, or trying to fix things on the go. But real change needs structure. It needs space and clarity.

That's where the Family Meeting idea comes in.

Don't wait for the moment of conflict to make a change. If the issue is fussiness at the table or sneaking biscuits from the cupboard, mealtime is not the moment to intervene. That just becomes nagging – and no one likes being told off mid-bite. Instead, make a mental note of the pattern you want to address, and write it down in a notebook reserved just for your Family Meetings.

This notebook becomes your shared space – a place to jot down topics, track progress, or record agreements. So when your child says, 'But I want another cookie!' you can gently show them the notebook and say, 'We agreed this last time – but if it's not working, let's write it down and talk about it at our next meeting.'

That way, change feels calm and collaborative – not reactive or punitive.

Put a regular date in the diary – once a week is good to start with – and stick to agreed times. And don't worry if your first few attempts feel a bit awkward. That's completely normal. With time, these meetings will feel more natural, and you'll likely start to see a real shift in the energy around the table.

Why Family Meetings Matter

Over time, these small, intentional gatherings can make a big difference – not just to how mealtimes unfold, but to the overall emotional tone of your home. They provide a safe space for talking and listening. Setting aside time for family conversations helps everyone feel more connected. These meetings give each person a chance to share their thoughts, worries, or ideas – and to feel truly listened to.

This builds trust, reduces misunderstandings, and helps children feel that their voice matters. They also help strengthen family bonds. When families talk openly about goals, challenges, or even small wins, they grow closer. These shared conversations create a sense of 'we're in this together.' When everyone has a role in making decisions, children feel more involved – and more willing to cooperate.

They also allow you to set clear expectations ahead of time, rather than reacting in the moment. You'll reduce arguments, avoid power struggles, and foster more harmony – all while giving your children a sense of fairness and clarity.

And they give you space to celebrate small wins. It's easy to focus on what needs fixing – but these meetings are also a chance to notice what's going well. Has someone tried a new food this week? Helped with the shopping or laid the table without being asked? When you make space to celebrate successes – even tiny ones – it lifts everyone's mood and encourages more of the same.

Are you a people-pleasing parent?

Another reason for having group family meetings is that it's not always easy to say 'no' to children, is it? We all want to raise well-mannered, well-adjusted children – but sometimes, in trying to keep the peace or avoid emotional drama, we slip into a habit of saying 'yes' too often. Not because we're lazy or inattentive, but because we're human.

This is what's often referred to as 'people-pleasing parenting' – a tendency to put short-term harmony above long-term growth. The intention is loving, but the outcome can be confusing for both parent and child.

There are many very valid reasons why saying 'no' can feel so difficult:

1. Avoiding Confrontation

Some parents are naturally conflict averse. After a long day, it's easier to give in than have a challenging debate.

2. Reacting to a Strict Childhood

If you grew up with overly firm rules, it's understandable that you want something softer for your own children. But softness without structure can leave children feeling unsure of where they stand.

3. Past Arguments That Left You Drained

When previous attempts at saying 'no' spiralled into shouting matches, it's natural to avoid repeating the pattern – especially if you're tired, overwhelmed, or busy.

4. Public Embarrassment

No parent enjoys being on the receiving end of backchat or tantrums in public. The urge to 'give in now, deal with it later' can feel overwhelming.

5. Wanting to Be Liked

Especially if you're going through a tough time yourself, your child's approval can feel extra comforting.

6. Parental Guilt

Whether due to work commitments, divorce, or time apart, guilt can sneak into parenting decisions – often disguised as generosity.

7. Emotional Discomfort

Watching your child become upset can trigger old wounds. It's not always their tears that are hard to manage – it's what those tears awaken in us.

In an earlier chapter, I asked you to think about the way you were fed as a child – I wonder if reading through this section will have enabled you to make some links with your own childhood.

Further along in this book, I teach you how to master the art of saying 'no' without actually using that word. It's all about the art of gentle persuasion – steering your child in the right direction.

Anchor Your Parenting in Values

The struggle to say 'no' in a weak moment, is the reason I encourage parents to get a clear sense of their family values – your family brand, so to speak. Businesses do this all the time. They know that it's important to get clear on their 'brand story' and put it front and centre on their website so everyone knows what the company stands for and the messages are clear.

It's the same for your family. Getting clear on your family story becomes your guiding identity and if the values have been discussed in a family group, then your children will start to become aware of them.

Keep your family values visible – on the fridge, in a notebook, wherever you'll see them. This is about how you want your children to turn out after 18 years of living with you.

When you know your values, decisions get easier. Once you have a structure or framework to work within, you don't need to debate every food rule or justify each change. You simply ask: does this fit with who we are?'

Defining your family values: What kind of family are we?

Pinning down a set of values can sometimes be a tricky exercise, so I'm going to help you here with a short questionnaire – take some time to reflect on these:

1. When it comes to feeding my child, what do I want to prioritise?
Examples: long-term health, home-cooked meals, calm mealtimes, positive body image, fewer ultra-processed foods.

2. What food-related habits or behaviours do I want my child to carry into adulthood?
Do you want them to know how to cook simple meals, recognise true hunger, enjoy fruit and veg, or eat without screens?

3. What role do I want food to play in our family life?
Is it a source of connection and comfort, or just fuel? What's the emotional tone of your meals – fun, rushed, relaxed, tense?

4. What am I trying to protect my child from?
Ultra-processed food dependency? Weight gain? Low energy? Eating disorders? Get specific.

5. What do I need to unlearn from my own childhood?
Were you made to clear your plate? Rewarded with sweets? Shamed for your appetite? This is your chance to rewrite that story.

Now turn your answers into 3–5 guiding values. Here are some examples to spark ideas:

- We eat for health and energy – not just taste.
- We teach our children how to listen to their bodies.
- We limit ultra-processed foods where we can – because we care.
- We make real food the norm – and treats just that: treats.

Setting Boundaries and Expectations

With values in place, it becomes easier to set consistent, reasonable boundaries. Children need to know what's expected of them, and when those expectations are clearly explained ahead of time (rather than in the heat of the moment), they're far more likely to cooperate.

Rather than reprimanding your child for refusing vegetables mid-meal, use your meeting time decision to back you up: '*Ah, we agreed at the Family Meeting that we'll always have at least one thing on the table that you like, and one thing that's new. You don't have to eat everything, but we'll be experimenting a little more from now on.*'

Making It Work for Your Family

Your meeting doesn't need to happen around a formal table. Choose a time and space that suits your family's energy:

- On a picnic blanket in the garden
- Sitting on cushions in the living room
- Around a campfire or lantern-lit evening walk
- A walk in the woods on a quiet weekend morning

Try mixing it up, especially if things start to feel repetitive. A new setting can spark creativity and open-mindedness.

Even how you sit can influence the tone of your discussion. If you're introducing a new idea that you want the whole family to visualise and support, sit in a row (theatre style), all facing the same direction. It helps everyone picture the same outcome.

If you're bouncing ideas around trying to find solutions to a challenge (like constant snacking or battles over dessert), sit around a table to encourage a flow of ideas from all directions.

Before you wrap up, take a moment to reflect as a family: What worked well today? What could we try differently next time?

Over time, these small, intentional gatherings will help you create a calmer, more connected family life – and most importantly, a shared story you can all be proud of.

Family Meeting Starter Checklist – Getting Set Up for Success

A little preparation now will make it far more likely that your family meetings actually happen – and keep happening.

1. Set a regular date and time
Choose a day that works for most of the family – Sunday mornings, Friday evenings, or whatever fits best. Consistency is key, even if the meetings are short. Aim for once a week to begin with.

2. Plan a month at a time
Look ahead and pencil in four weekly meetings now. Add them to the family calendar or a shared phone app – whatever helps keep everyone on track.

3. Choose your location

Decide where your meetings will take place: be open to switching it up now and then to keep things fresh.

4. Create a simple agenda

Just a few points will do:
- Something that went well this week
- A challenge or issue to solve
- Anything new to try (e.g., a different vegetable, new meal routine)
- A fun or silly question to lighten the mood

5.   Get a notebook or family journal

Use this to jot down meeting notes, agreements, goals, or even drawings from younger children. It creates a record of progress and shows everyone their input is valued.

6. Set up a Weekly Menu Board

Use a whiteboard, chalkboard, or a sheet on the fridge. In each meeting, talk about what meals are coming up. Let children help plan – they're more likely to eat what they've helped choose.

7. Make it fun

Keep the mood light. Add music, snacks, or a small game to begin. If it feels like a chore, it won't last. If it feels like connection, it will.

8. Keep it short

15–20 minutes is plenty. End while everyone's still engaged, and leave space to build on things next time.

9. Be flexible, not perfect

If a week gets missed or the conversation goes off-topic, don't worry. You're building a habit, not a flawless record.

When families sit down together to talk things through, it becomes easier to agree on shared values – and once those are clear, setting boundaries feels less like a battle and more like teamwork.

WORDS THAT WORK

The Language of Persuasion and Influence

Now that you've started planning *how* you'll introduce change to your child, it's time to consider something equally important: *the language you use to talk about it.*

In my bestselling book *'Words That Work: How to Get Kids to Do Almost Anything'*, I go into detail about the power of language – and how changing just a few simple words can be the difference between resistance and cooperation. If you'd like to dive deeper, that book is a great companion to this chapter.

Language has an almost hypnotic effect on children – especially when they're young. Their minds absorb messages quickly and literally, so what you say (and how you say it) can have a surprisingly strong influence.

The good news?

A few simple shifts in the way you speak can dramatically increase your child's willingness to cooperate – and help you feel calmer and more confident as a parent.

When it comes to making change stick, the words you use matter. A lot. Let me show you a few examples of how changing words can create different outcomes.

1. Say What You Do Want – Not What You Don't
Children respond better to positive direction. Instead of telling them what **not** to do (which often creates the wrong image in their mind), help them focus on what to do.

Compare these statements:

'Let's leave the room nice and tidy'
rather than:
'Don't leave your room in a mess'

'Let's sit at the table as quiet as mice today'
rather than:
'Stop mucking around and making noise'

'Remember to walk calmly and slowly'
rather than:
'Don't run!'

'Remember to have your sports bag ready for tomorrow'
rather than:
'Don't forget your sports bag!'

Negative instructions often plant the very idea you want to avoid. Saying 'don't forget' creates a mental image of forgetting – which makes it more likely to happen. Instead, give your child a clear, positive image to follow.

2. Avoid Words That Block Motivation

It's common to create obstacles in someone's mind without realising it. Phrases like:

'You must...'
'You should...'
'You could...'

These phrases often carry heaviness or hesitation. They sound vague, non-committal – and they feel that way too. Think about how these words have an effect on your own motivation.

'I must sort out the cupboards' feels like a chore.
But *'I'm going to sort out the cupboards on Tuesday'* feels planned and manageable.

'I ought to walk the dog' feels like guilt.
But *'I'll walk the dog at 11am this morning'* creates momentum and a positive image.

The same goes when speaking to your child. Instead of:
'You must eat some vegetables'
say:
'Let's add a little bit of broccoli to your plate today – just a taste to start with.'

Instead of commanding or correcting, you're calmly guiding. You're inviting, not insisting – and that makes all the difference.

3. Use the Illusion of Choice

Another powerful language tool is to offer choices – but cleverly.
By giving your child two options (both of which you approve of), you're helping them feel a sense of control while gently guiding them in the direction you want.

For example:

'Do you want to work on your school project *today or tomorrow*?'

'Would you like to pack your bag *before or after* supper?'

'Do you want to wear the *blue or the red* t-shirt?'

'Which vegetable would you like to try first – *the peas or the carrots*?'

Even better, you can turn a problem into a practical plan:

'So, what I'm hearing is that there are three things stopping you from doing your homework: you're hungry, you've lost your pencil, and you need to check with your friend about the assignment.

Which one do you want to sort out first? Obviously, you can't do all three at the same time – so let's choose one, fix that, and move on from there.'

You've reframed the challenge as a series of manageable steps – and let your child feel they're steering the process.

Tip: Don't overuse this technique with very young children – it can lose its magic if repeated too often. But used sparingly, it's a brilliant tool to keep up your sleeve.

4. Never 'Try' anything

Read through this powerful exercise to see how one tiny little word can so easily create a negative picture and hold you back. It's not always easy to read a set of instructions and follow them yourself, so test it out on friends and family first and see what results you get.

Ask them to close their eyes and slowly, give them these instructions and then, have them do the same to you.

1. Close your eyes and see in your imagination a door.
2. Notice the colour of the door and say the colour out loud.

3. Open the door.
4. When you have opened the door, open your eyes.

PAUSE

5. Now close your eyes again and see in your imagination a door.
6. Notice the colour of the door and say the colour out loud.
7. *Try* to open the door.
8. And when you've opened the door, you can open your eyes again.

- What difference did you find between the first door and the second door?
- Were the doors the same colour, or different?
- Did they have handles, locks or bolts?
- Were the handles on the same side?
- Did the doors open slowly or quickly?

As you'll discover, when you use the word 'try' people tend to find opening the door very difficult, or they'll not be able to do it at all. It's quite incredible how such a small word can have such a big impact, but it does. By automatically suggesting that whatever it is you're planning to do is going to be a struggle, it becomes just that.

This is an interesting exercise and will probably make you think back to your own childhood. How many times did someone say to you; 'as long as you *try*, that's all that matters', or '*try* your best', or 'just *try* and have a go', or best of all '*try* your hardest!'

Twice in one sentence, it has been suggested to you that you're going to struggle.

How different would the results have been if you had been given positive directions rather than those negative ones that held you back?

'Try' is definitely a word to avoid using with your kids – and will explain why each time you say 'just *try* one mouthful', you get met with resistance. Think about it – if the food was delicious, you'd be encouraging your child to have more than one mouthful, wouldn't you? '*Try just one*' must mean it's not very tasty – surely?

The Energy Around the Table

Sometimes mealtimes go wrong simply because... well, you're expecting them to. Children are incredibly perceptive – they don't need you to say a word. They can read your body language, pick up on the tension in the room, and before you know it, they're playing up.

Meanwhile, some parents seem to float through family meals with ease. They'll say things like, 'I'm so lucky – my kids eat everything I put in front of them.'

Really? Honestly?

I remember feeling a pang of jealousy hearing those comments – until I found myself invited to one of their homes for dinner. What did I see? Tantrums, refusals, fussiness – the usual.

But here's the difference: the parent was calm, unfazed, and completely in control. To her, things were going just fine. And to be fair, they probably were – most of the time. She was focusing on the 80% that went well – and simply letting the rest pass by without giving it too much energy.

If, on the other hand, you're someone who is focused on the 20% that doesn't go to plan, you'll start to feel like every mealtime is a struggle. And when that becomes your story, you'll start attracting more of that energy.

You'll find yourself complaining about mealtimes to your partner, your parents, your friends – and often within earshot of the very children you're frustrated with. (And yes, they are always listening.) Eventually, the message they hear is: 'My kids always mess up mealtimes. They're so noisy, fussy, never eat their vegetables'. And so, the cycle continues.

But here's the good news: when you shift the way you think about your mealtimes, your family's experience of them will begin to shift too.

Avoid using words like '*always*' and '*never*'. Use '*sometimes*' instead.

Change the energy, and the experience changes with it.

Moving Forward – A Foundation for Change

By now, you're getting a clearer idea of how to map out your priorities, gather your family around the table, and start using the kind of words that foster cooperation, not resistance. We're doing the groundwork – and that's no small thing.

These simple tools – a calm meeting, a clearer message, a more encouraging tone – will form the foundation for everything that comes next. They may seem subtle, but they create powerful shifts in energy, behaviour, and family connection.

So now, we move into the heart of the work: the everyday challenges. From fussy eating to snack food cravings, from food anxiety to rising weight issues – the next chapters will help you navigate these with practical strategies, gentle interventions, and insight from my therapy room.

Wherever you start, remember this: You don't have to fix everything at once. You just need to begin – one conversation, one habit, one meal at a time.

Let's move on and explore the specific challenges – and what to do when they show up in your home.

READ MORE: My book '*Words that Work: How to get kids to do almost anything*' has more examples of how to use the language of persuasion effectively. Visit: www.aliciaeaton.co.uk for more details.

8

FUSSY EATING CHALLENGES

I Understand Your Pain

Let me start by saying: I've been there. By that, I don't mean the kind of fussy eating where a child refuses peas one day and then eats three spoonfuls the next. I'm talking about the kind that dominates family life. The kind that leaves you worrying constantly about nutrition, social occasions, and what might happen if your child is ever offered something unfamiliar.

My son, George, was that child. He was a sicky baby – unsettled from the very start. Feeding was always a struggle. Even during the weaning stage, he rejected most foods and gagged easily.

By the time he was three, we were referred to the local hospital for weekly sessions with a psychologist. That's how difficult things had become. And did those sessions help? Honestly – no. Not in the slightest.

Like so many parents, we were told he'd 'grow out of it,' but that didn't match the day-to-day reality of trying to feed a child who wouldn't go near most foods – and reacted so strongly to certain smells that he would physically retch if he even caught a whiff of pizza or fried food.

I still remember the mortifying moment at a hotel breakfast buffet when the smell in the dining room became too much for him and…… well, you can imagine the rest.

He wouldn't eat meat, eggs, cheese, or butter. Bread? No. Pasta or rice? Absolutely not. And vegetables – just peas and sweetcorn. He wouldn't even sit at a table if there were sausages or bacon nearby. Yet, curiously, he'd eat pancakes on Pancake Day. He was a complete mystery.

His list of acceptable foods was short: fish fingers, peas, sweetcorn, croissants, crisps, apples, oranges, lemons (skins and all), and hot chocolate made with fresh milk. That was it – for years. He even refused to eat lunch at school because they didn't allow packed lunches, only cooked meals. So he just didn't eat. I think he spent most of his childhood feeling hungry.

And yet, despite his extreme fussiness, he was determined, focused – but deeply anxious about being 'tricked' into eating something unfamiliar. He'd panic about going anywhere new in case he was offered strange food – and it's fair to say, a few tantrums followed.

After several exhausting years of battles and arguments, I realised that for things to change, I had to change first.

By the time he was eight, I stopped trying to fix him. I stopped making it a problem – and, guess what, the problem started to go away. I made him a promise: I would never make him eat something he didn't want to. In fact, I would stop encouraging him to try new foods altogether. We'd stop talking about it.

But in return, he had to respect the mealtime routine – eat politely, use cutlery, sit at the table, stop making a fuss, no drama and no kicking off in an embarrassing way at other people's houses. That was the deal.

I would stop doing what I was doing – but he had to stop the protests too. We shook hands on it.

Of course, he continued eating his narrow range of foods – including fish fingers on Christmas Day – but the tension lifted. Mealtimes became calmer. And that was the start of things getting better.

Years later, when George was thirteen, something astonishing happened. He watched someone eating a steak and casually asked why I'd never given him meat. I stared at him. 'Because you told me you didn't like meat,' I replied. He looked baffled. 'That's ridiculous. I've always liked meat.'

Kids – so infuriating! And so the repertoire expanded: steak, roast chicken, and eventually, other foods followed.

Today, George is all grown up. He still won't eat a sandwich (because of the butter), but he'll happily devour a hummus wrap. He adores salmon, sea bass, cous cous with roasted vegetables, avocados, falafel, and steamed broccoli. He won't go near sausages or bacon. He's practically a health nut – passionate about eating well and staying fit. I admire his discipline, and yes, I sometimes find it a little irritating too!

Looking back, I realise that all those years of struggle weren't just about the food. They were about deep sensory sensitivities and I believe, the hypermobility that runs in our family has something to do with this as well – I discuss this in more detail in the next chapter about sensory issues.

While it felt impossible at times, what made the biggest difference was creating a calm, structured environment – and letting go of the pressure.

So if you're reading this now, and feeling desperate or defeated, please know: I see you. I understand. And I promise, it can get better – not by forcing change, but by creating the conditions where change becomes possible.

Creating a Positive Mealtime Environment

Before we explore strategies or introduce new foods, the first step is to make mealtimes a calm, pleasant, and pressure-free experience. Here are some simple, effective ways to do just that:

1. Make Mealtimes a Family Affair
Try to eat together as often as possible. Sitting down as a family helps children feel included, valued, and more open to trying what's on their plate. Avoid hovering or using this time to get chores done. Be present. Eat with them.

2. Set the Scene
Create a calm and inviting atmosphere. Use soft background music, set the table with real crockery and napkins (ditch the plastic and cartoon characters), and add small touches like flowers or a candle. These little rituals help signal that this is a special time to connect, not just fuel up and dash off.

3. Give Children a Role
Involve your child in setting the table or pouring water. These simple tasks offer structure and routine, giving them a sense of ownership before the food even arrives. Helping out also gently eases them into the mealtime experience.

4. Plan the Week Together
Sit down once a week and create a meal plan as a family – use your

'Family Meeting' for this. Let each child choose a favourite meal and agree together what will be cooked each day. Stick the plan on the fridge. This reduces complaints, increases predictability, and teaches children that everyone's preferences matter – not just theirs.

5. Keep Things Predictable
Serve meals at regular times, with as few surprises as possible. Children feel safer and more regulated when they know what to expect. A calm mealtime rhythm supports appetite and mood.

6. Focus on Connection, Not Correction
Mealtimes should never be the place to discipline, lecture, or scold. If you need to address a behaviour, do it outside the meal – ideally in your weekly Family Meeting. At the table, focus on conversation, connection, and keeping the mood light.

7. Use Starters and Tasting Plates
Put small ramekins of veg sticks and dips on the table while you finish cooking. Children can nibble without pressure. Or create a 'tasting plate' with tiny dollops of colourful purees and let everyone try them, one by one, as a game.

8. Keep the Mood Upbeat
Avoid complaints or negativity at the table. Create a family tradition of sharing one piece of good news each night. Or take turns reading a joke from a book. Positive emotions boost appetite – especially for children who are anxious or avoidant around food.

9. Respect Their Pace
It's tempting to give up on a food once it's been rejected. But just because they won't eat it today doesn't mean they never will. Keep offering – without pressure. Touching, smelling, or exploring food is progress. Trust the process.

The Gentle Compromise: Offering a Side Dish or Starter

Sometimes, you know before the meal even hits the table that one child is going to push their plate away. Maybe it's fish night and your youngest hates the smell. Maybe it's curry, and one child finds even mild spice unbearable. This doesn't mean you have to abandon your plan or cook a second meal. It just means you can plan ahead with a small act of compromise.

When you're introducing a new or less-favoured dish, try offering a simple side dish or starter that you know your child is comfortable with. This could be something as basic as:
- a small bowl of chopped cucumber or plain carrot sticks,
- a slice of buttered bread,
- a handful of plain pasta,
- or even a boiled egg or plain rice on the side.

You're not replacing the meal, you're adding something familiar. This approach does a few things at once:

It reduces anxiety: the child sees something safe on the table and doesn't feel ambushed.

It builds trust: they learn that even when they don't love the main dish, there's something there for them.

It eases pressure: children are more likely to try new things when they're not starving or overwhelmed.

You can talk about it at your family meeting: 'Some nights, we'll be having meals that not everyone loves. On those nights, we'll try having a small starter or side that makes it easier. It's not a second dinner – it's just a way to make sure you don't feel left out.'

Over time, the goal is not to rely on this forever, but to use it as a stepping stone – until your child becomes more flexible and confident around different foods. The difference here is that you decide what the side dish is – it's a parent-led compromise, not a negotiation. And that's the key.

Sensory Exploration – the Montessori way

Let me introduce you to some activities that are deeply rooted in Montessori principles and are the kind of exercises I would give children when I was running my own school. Designed to refine and enhance the senses during their developmental stage, they're much more than fun games – and I feel, will help your child to become more comfortable with different types of food.

Activity 1: Show and Tell (Food Exploration Party)
- Invite friends over and ask each one to bring an unusual food item.
- Let children explore the appearance, feel, and smell of each item, and share what they know or wonder about where it comes from.
- Look up the origin together online and explore the culture behind it. This collaborative learning atmosphere makes food discovery more exciting and social.

Activity 2: Guess the Food (Sensory Discovery Game)
- Place a blindfold over your child's eyes and invite them to touch, smell, and explore a mystery food item.
- Ask them to describe its texture, shape, and scent.
- If your child is uncomfortable wearing a blindfold, use a drawstring bag – they can reach in and feel the item without seeing it. This helps develop tactile awareness and builds comfort with new foods through non-threatening, playful interaction.

Activity 3: Smelling Jars (Montessori-Style Scent Matching)
- Use six identical containers with lids that have small holes (salt and pepper pots are ideal).
- Create three matching pairs by placing scented items (e.g. coffee granules, cinnamon sticks, mint leaves) inside. Another option is to use cotton wool balls with drops of essence on them.
- Invite your child to sniff each one in turn and find the matching pairs.
- Reveal the answers after guessing. This builds scent discrimination and reduces aversions to smells.

Helping Children Tune In – Mindfully

Mindfulness isn't just about sitting still with your eyes closed – it's about helping children slow down and notice what's happening in their bodies. When it comes to food, this can be a game-changer.

Simple, playful mindfulness techniques encourage children to become more intuitive eaters – to recognise when they're hungry, when they've had enough, and what their body actually needs. These little moments of awareness can reduce anxiety, build confidence, and gently guide children away from mindless snacking or mealtime battles.

1. The Slow Bite Game
Goal: To teach children to feel more comfortable exploring new foods.
How to Play: Sit with your child and take one small piece of food – a slice of apple, a square of toast, a raisin.
Say: Let's see who can eat this the slowest!
Ask:
- What does it look like? Notice the colour, shape, texture.
- What does it smell like?
- Can you hear it when you break it or take a bite?

- Let it sit on your tongue for a moment – what's the first thing you notice?
- Chew slowly – how many chews can you do before swallowing?
- Make it playful. You're not teaching – you're exploring together.

2. Colour and Crunch

Goal: To bring awareness to food through the senses – especially sight and sound.

How to Play: Create a mini rainbow plate – a few tiny pieces of colourful fruits/veg (e.g., cucumber, pepper, blueberry, carrot).

Say: Let's look at all the colours before we start.

Ask:

- What does red taste like?
- What colour do you think will crunch the loudest?

Make a mini score sheet for:

- Loudest crunch
- Juiciest bite
- Most surprising texture
- Favourite colour to eat
- This gently builds a positive and curious attitude toward food – especially healthy ones.

3. Tummy Talk

Goal: To help children connect with hunger/fullness signals.

How to Play: Before a meal or snack, sit quietly for one minute.

Say: Put your hands on your tummy. Close your eyes.

Ask: Is it saying'

- I'm hungry'?
- I'm not sure?
- I'm full?

You can add a little story:

Imagine your tummy is a traffic light. What colour is it showing?

- Red = Full

- Yellow = Unsure
- Green = Hungry

This helps a child pause and listen inwardly – a skill many adults struggle with.

4. The Tiny Turtle Game

Goal: Create a calm, mindful mealtime through gentle fun.

How to Play: Explain that today you'll be eating like tiny turtles – slow and steady. Turtles never rush. We're going to:

- Take one bite at a time.
- Chew slowly.
- Put our knives and forks down between bites.
- If you want to speak, raise a turtle flipper (hand!) and wait.
- You can even print a little turtle card and pop it on the table as a reminder. A lovely one for family meals where things usually get rushed.

IN THE THERAPY ROOM

Two Brothers, One Suggestion – Eating Out Without Fear

I was contacted by a mother of two boys, aged eight and ten, who'd long struggled with their limited eating habits – particularly when it came to situations outside the home. While Mum was able to manage their fussiness in a familiar kitchen, anything unfamiliar – restaurants, friend's houses, holidays – would quickly unravel into chaos. The boys would cry, refuse to eat, and sometimes even shout if something unfamiliar appeared on their plate.

It wasn't that they were being difficult for the sake of it. The distress they felt was very real. But understandably, it had taken a toll on the whole family. Holidays had become something to dread rather than enjoy, and the family often opted for villa rentals with kitchens just to avoid restaurant outings altogether.

But now, the stakes had changed. Their father – a successful movie director – was about to attend a major international film festival, where his latest feature was being showcased. There were high hopes that he would win an award.

The family would be travelling together for the full event. That meant hotel stays, formal dinners, and several high-profile meals in restaurants where both boys would be expected to attend and, ideally, sit and eat without drama. As Mum put it to me, 'This is too important. We can't have them kicking off at every table. It's not an option this time.'

Interestingly, the request to try hypnotherapy had come not from the mother, but from the boys themselves. 'I want to be hypnotised,' the older one declared, having clearly heard about it somewhere and decided it sounded like the solution he needed. The younger one agreed. The mother asked if I could hypnotise them both – at the same time.

I hesitated, initially. Although they were brothers and shared the same challenges on the surface, it was likely that each boy's anxiety came from a different place. One might be reacting to certain smells or textures, the other perhaps responding to past experiences of embarrassment or overwhelm. Hypnosis, at its' best, is highly personal. But I also knew the power of suggestion, and more importantly, the power of sibling connection. So I agreed.

They sat side by side as we began the session. Rather than trying to tailor two different visualisations or interventions, I used a carefully planted suggestion – one that allowed them to create their own shift, at their own pace:

'Now I don't know which one of you it will be – the one who first lets this old problem go, and finds himself feeling calm and comfortable, even in new places and unfamiliar restaurants. But I do know that whoever it is, the other one will follow quickly after... almost as if one brother's calm is a signpost for the other.'

That was it. There was no pressure. No specific food they had to eat. No challenge to conquer. Just an invitation to shift.

A few weeks later, I received a message from their mother. She was delighted. The boys had attended every restaurant meal during the festival, and not only had they managed to sit through without complaint – they had enjoyed the experience. She told me that when one of them had shown a flicker of nerves, he instinctively looked to the other. And if his brother looked calm, that was all he needed. It was as though each one was waiting to discover whether he was the first or the second. And whichever role he stepped into, he felt reassured.

As it happens, their father did win an award at the festival. And while the trophy was a proud moment for the family, the real triumph may have been much quieter: two brothers, sitting side by side at the table, calm and confident in themselves – and in each other.

A gentle thought to take with you:

Sometimes change doesn't come through effort, but through quiet suggestion – a gentle nudge that allows a child's own mind to do the work. And when siblings are involved, the transformation can be doubled. One child's calm becomes the other's confidence. One small shift creates space for another. When we trust that connection, and allow suggestion to work subtly rather than forcefully, even long-held struggles can begin to soften.

If you take just one thing from this chapter, let it be this: change doesn't happen overnight – but it does happen. Whether your child is mildly hesitant or deeply avoidant around food, progress is possible when you shift the focus away from pressure and towards calm, consistent structure. You don't need to win every mealtime. You simply need empathy, patience, and faith that, in time, your child will grow in confidence.

In the next chapter, we'll explore how deeper sensory issues and neurodivergent traits can affect eating behaviours – and how to support children who may need a different kind of approach altogether.

READ MORE: My book *First Aid for your Child's Mind* has more advice for helping children overcome anxiety. Visit www.aliciaeaton. co.uk for more details.

9

FOOD ANXIETY & SENSORY SENSITIVITIES

When eating feels difficult

Children interpret their world through their senses – what they see, hear, feel, touch, smell, and taste. To a greater or lesser extent, this process works pretty much the same way for most children. But it can also sometimes lead to behaviour that puzzles or even frustrates us.

You may notice your child reacts strongly to certain sounds, textures, or environments – or perhaps they seem to seek out constant movement or noise. These are often signs of two distinct sensory styles: sensory-sensitive and sensory-seeking.

A 'sensory-sensitive' child tends to experience the world as louder, brighter, or more overwhelming than others might. They might find scratchy clothing unbearable or struggle in busy places.

On the other hand, a 'sensory-seeking' child is driven to seek more stimulation. These are the children who love jumping, crashing, or fiddling with anything in sight.

Understanding these differences can be especially helpful when it comes to eating habits. What we often call fussy eating may in fact be a reflection of a child's sensory sensitivities.

For a sensory-sensitive child, the texture of mashed potato might feel just as unpleasant as a scratchy jumper. The smell of cooked vegetables might seem overpowering, or certain food combinations might feel simply 'wrong' in their mouth. These children aren't being difficult – they're reacting to sensory input that feels too intense.

In contrast, sensory-seeking children may be more adventurous with food, enjoying strong flavours, crunchy textures, or even spicy dishes, because they're naturally drawn to more stimulation. Recognising where your child falls on this sensory spectrum can make mealtimes feel less like a battleground and more like an opportunity to gently support their unique needs.

For Sensory-Sensitive Children (who may be fussy eaters)

These children may be overwhelmed by textures, smells, or the way food looks or feels in the mouth.

1. Start with what feels safe.
Stick with foods your child already tolerates, then make small, gradual changes – like cutting it a different way, warming it slightly, or introducing a new brand.

2. Deconstruct meals.
Avoid mixed textures or foods that are 'touching.' Serve ingredients separately – think plain pasta, cheese on the side, cucumber slices rather than a salad.

3. Respect their reactions without pressure.

Saying things like, 'It's on your plate, just you can explore it,' helps reduce anxiety and gives them a sense of control.

4. Use the 'tiny taste' rule.

Encourage a no-pressure taste – literally the tip of a tongue. Over time, this can help build tolerance to new flavours or textures.

5. Involve them in prep.

Let your child help with washing, stirring, or arranging food – even if they don't eat it. Exposure without expectation can be powerful.

6. Consider non-food sensory experiences.

Messy play with sand, water, or play dough can gently build tolerance for different textures without the pressure of eating.

For Sensory-Seeking Children (who may eat a lot, fast, or prefer strong flavours)

These children may crave bold tastes and crunchy or chewy textures – and may have a harder time recognising when they're full.

1. Offer texture-rich, chewy foods.

Raw carrots, apples, bagels, or dried fruit can satisfy their need for oral input in a way that supports regulation.

2. Provide strong, bold flavours (within reason).

They may prefer tangy, spicy, or sour foods. You can offer variety through dips, seasoning, or more flavourful options – just watch for overindulgence.

3. Slow things down.

Use small cutlery or fun routines (like 'chew five times before the next bite') to encourage mindful eating.

4. Offer food in short bursts.
Instead of large portions, try smaller amounts more frequently throughout the day to avoid overwhelm or grazing.

5. Use crunchy snacks for self-regulation.
Sometimes a crunchy snack can help with focus and calm – use strategically, like before school or a tricky transition.

Hypermobility: The Hidden Link to Mealtime Struggles

It's not always easy to spot the deeper reasons behind a child's fussy eating, especially when they've been labelled as 'just picky.' But for some children, particularly those with hypermobility, their relationship with food may have been shaped by discomfort long before they could speak a word.

Hypermobility is a condition where joints move beyond the normal range of motion, often due to unusually stretchy ligaments, which can lead to pain, fatigue, or instability. The term **Hypermobility Spectrum Disorder (HSD)** is now more commonly used to better reflect the range and complexity of symptoms people may experience.

Hypermobility doesn't only affect joints – it can also influence how internal systems function, including the digestive tract. This means that a child who seems to reject food might not be simply difficult, but rather reacting to real sensations of pain or unease.

Many hypermobile children are born with lax connective tissue, which can lead to issues like reflux, poor gut motility, or a sensitive gag reflex. For these children, eating isn't simply about nourishment – it can feel overwhelming or even unpleasant. It's not hard to see how, over time, they may come to associate mealtimes with discomfort, and begin to avoid certain foods or textures altogether. Add in a naturally cautious or anxious temperament – something that's often seen in children with sensory sensitivities – and their world of food can quickly become very small.

But the good news is that this cycle can be gently shifted. By understanding the physical reasons behind a child's reactions, we can begin to take the pressure off and create a more positive, supportive environment around eating.

I'm pleased that today, Hypermobility is getting more attention as it's a condition that runs in my family. It's only now that my children are all grown up that I can see how it has manifested itself – one of my sons can easily pop his joints out of their sockets.

And I do believe this is the cause of my son George's fussy eating. He's very hypermobile and it would explain his constant sickiness as a baby and the endless nights of crying – for months on end. As he was my first child and I was a young mother, I didn't really know what was normal at the time. It was only later, with two more children under my belt, that I could see how very wrong things were for him at the time.

There are some positive aspects to having hypermobility though – I now understand why I always gave birth so easily. My second son arrived in just one hour and I still remember the midwife shouting at me that my child would never forgive me if I allowed it to be born in the hospital car park, so I was to cross my legs and hang on till we were inside. It was a race against time!

Understanding ARFID: When Fussy Eating Becomes Something More Serious

ARFID – short for **Avoidant/Restrictive Food Intake Disorder** – is a relatively new, clinically recognised eating disorder that goes beyond typical childhood fussy eating. While many children go through phases of rejecting certain foods, ARFID is marked by an extreme, persistent avoidance that can lead to serious nutritional, developmental, and psychological consequences.

Children with this disorder will avoid or restrict food, not because of body image worries, but for other reasons. It might be due to sensitivity to textures, smells or tastes, a fear of being sick or choking, or simply not feeling very interested in eating at all.

They may eat only a very narrow range of foods – often 'safe' foods like plain pasta, toast, or particular brands – and experience high anxiety when presented with anything outside their comfort zone.

ARFID was officially added to the DSM-5 (Diagnostic and Statistical Manual of Mental Disorders, 5th Edition) in 2013, marking it as a distinct diagnosis separate from eating disorders such as anorexia or bulimia. Before this, such behaviours were often misunderstood or misdiagnosed.

In the UK, diagnoses of ARFID have increased fivefold over five years, according to the eating disorder charity Beat. While exact figures are still emerging, it's estimated that ARFID affects up to 5% of children – though some experts believe the true number could be higher due to underdiagnosis or confusion with extreme fussy eating.

ARFID is being seen across a wide range of ages, but it's most commonly identified in children and adolescents, particularly those with: autism spectrum conditions; anxiety disorders; sensory processing difficulties.

It's important for parents and practitioners to understand that sensory-based avoidance isn't behavioural defiance – it's a sensory overload. Children aren't being awkward – they're trying to protect themselves from an experience that feels overwhelming or even painful. With the right support, progress is possible. But it starts with understanding.

The Psycho-Sensory Approach to Eating

As we've seen, eating isn't just about hunger – it's a fully immersive experience involving touch, taste, smell, sight, and even sound. From the crunch of a crisp to the smoothness of chocolate... the cool fizz of a drink to the cosy warmth of toast – food speaks to us through texture, temperature, smell, sound, and sight.

And that's why taking a psycho-sensory approach makes sense. The term is grounded in neuroscience. It's based on the understanding that our sensory systems are directly connected to emotional regulation centres in the brain – especially the amygdala (which processes fear and anxiety) and the prefrontal cortex (involved in decision-making and self-control).

I've designed this **Psycho-Sensory Eating Profile** – a simple tool for parents and carers to help you spot your child's unique sensory preferences when it comes to food. Just as we recognise different learning styles – visual, auditory, kinaesthetic – children also have eating styles. Some are drawn to crunch, others to softness. Some need strong flavours or warm foods to feel settled, while others are easily overwhelmed by certain textures or smells.

This profile is suitable for all children – not just those with sensory sensitivities or neurodivergent traits. In fact, most adults will recognise their own preferences too!

It will give you a new way to look at your child's eating habits – one that replaces frustration with understanding and helps you support your child with confidence and compassion.

You can complete the profile here – and then match it up with my suggestions for '**Psycho-sensory swaps**'.

The Psycho-Sensory Eating Profile™

1. What does your child love eating or snacking on?
(✓ all that apply)
- ☐ Crunchy things – crisps, toast, raw veg, crackers
- ☐ Smooth or creamy foods – yogurt, mousse, mashed potato
- ☐ Chewy foods – bagels, dried fruit, gummy sweets
- ☐ Cold foods – ice cream, smoothies, frozen fruit
- ☐ Warm, soft foods – porridge, toast, soup
- ☐ Tangy or strong flavours – pickles, citrus, spice
- ☐ Bland, beige foods – plain pasta, dry cereal, white bread

2. How does your child react to new foods or unfamiliar textures?
- ☐ Recoils at the feel or look of certain foods
- ☐ Touches or plays with food before eating
- ☐ Smells everything before trying
- ☐ Reluctant to mix foods (e.g. stew or salad)
- ☐ More curious than cautious – likes to explore
- ☐ Seeks intense flavours or temperatures

3. What sensory experiences do they enjoy outside of food?

☐ Playing with sand, kinetic toys, or messy textures

☐ Fidgeting or chewing (clothes, pencils, sleeves)

☐ Soothing with warmth – blankets, baths

☐ Seeking cold – ice cubes, fridge door, fans

☐ Enjoying bold smells – perfumes, food, candles

☐ Avoiding noise, mess, or strong smells

4. How do they usually behave around mealtimes?

☐ Eats fast and asks for more

☐ Eats slowly and picks at textures

☐ Often 'not hungry' but loves snacks

☐ Asks for food based on mood (tired, sad, bored)

☐ Needs quiet, calm to eat well

☐ Eats better when food is separated and predictable

Matching the Sensory Profile to Expand Food Choices

Once you've completed the psycho-sensory eating profile, you'll have a clearer picture of your child's sensory preferences when it comes to food – whether they favour crunchy textures, smooth consistencies, hot or cold sensations.

This insight can be incredibly useful if your child struggles with food anxiety or ARFID. Rather than trying to introduce entirely unfamiliar foods, use this profile to find similar-feeling alternatives. If a child already enjoys cold, smooth foods like yogurt, they may be more willing to try something like chilled hummus or a fruit smoothie. Matching new foods to their preferred sensory experience gives you a better chance of expanding their repertoire – gently, and with less resistance.

Psycho-Sensory Swaps: What is my mouth looking for?

CRUNCHY: I like crunching – it helps me wake up or calm down.
Choose:
- Carrot sticks
- Apple slices
- Cucumber rounds
- Air-popped popcorn
- Wholegrain crackers

CHEWY: I feel like chewing and chomping – it helps me focus or feel strong.
Choose:
- Dried fruit (unsweetened)
- Wholegrain toast or bagel
- Rice cakes
- Homemade energy balls
- Sugar-free gum (if age-appropriate)

SOFT/FLUFFY: I want something gentle and comforting in my mouth.
Choose:
- Banana
- Mashed sweet potato
- Steamed veggies
- Scrambled egg
- Wholemeal sandwich with soft filling

COLD: I want a cool feeling – maybe I need to refresh or chill out.
Choose:
- Frozen fruit
- Yogurt
- Smoothie ice pop
- Cold water with mint or lemon
- Chilled melon or cucumber

CREAMY/SMOOTH: I want something silky or soothing – like a food hug.

Choose:
- Plain yogurt with fruit
- Avocado mash
- Oat porridge
- Hummus
- Smooth soup

TANGY/ZINGY: I want a burst of flavour – something to wake up my taste buds!

Choose:
- Orange, pineapple, or kiwi
- Lemon/lime water
- Pickles (low salt)
- Berries
- Cherry tomatoes

WARM: I want something cosy and warm – it helps me feel safe or relaxed.

Choose:
- Warm milk or oat milk
- Porridge or oatmeal
- Toast with nut butter
- Warm veggie soup
- Baked sweet potato

STICKY: I want something gooey or stretchy – something to play with in my mouth.

Choose:
- Dates
- Natural peanut or almond butter
- Melted cheese on wholegrain toast
- Raisins
- Mashed banana on rice cakes

SALTY: I'm craving something savoury or strong-tasting.
Choose:
– Lightly salted popcorn
– Wholegrain crackers with cheese
– Olives (in moderation)
– Hard-boiled egg with a sprinkle of salt
– Roasted chickpeas

SPICY: I want a little heat or kick – something exciting for my tongue!
Choose:
– Mild salsa with veggie sticks
– Spiced hummus
– Peppery crackers
– Cucumber with a sprinkle of chili powder (if age-appropriate)
– Light curry-flavoured lentil soup

IN THE THERAPY ROOM

Fear, Food, and Feeling Safe Again

16 year old Daniel came to see me after a particularly difficult experience on a family holiday. While dining out, he'd eaten sushi at a seafood restaurant – something he'd never had before – and shortly after, suffered a nasty bout of food poisoning. Although his body recovered, the emotional imprint lingered far longer.

By the time I met him, Daniel had become incredibly anxious about eating, not just in restaurants, but at home too. He was now examining his food closely before eating, sometimes holding it up to the light, checking it over, and asking his parents to confirm – again and again – that it had been prepared hygienically.

What had started as a reaction to one upsetting incident had now evolved into something more consuming. Mealtimes, understandably, had become a challenge – for him and for the whole family. They had already sought help from a psychologist who, well-meaning as they were, may have unintentionally intensified Daniel's fears. In their first session, the psychologist laid out a treatment plan, explaining that after six sessions, he would be able to eat sushi again.

For Daniel, this was the very opposite of reassurance. He didn't want to eat sushi. Ever again. That food had become firmly associated with a frightening experience, and now someone was telling him that recovery meant repeating it. Understandably, he felt backed into a corner.

What made matters more pressing was something new and important in Daniel's life – he'd just started seeing a girl he really liked. She'd invited him over for dinner to meet her family, and instead of feeling excited, Daniel was terrified. He was scared he'd panic at the table, that he'd feel sick, or worse – have to run to the bathroom. And so, he and his parents came to see me.

We spent two hours together. No pressure. No 'end goals' like eating sushi. Just calm, focused work around what Daniel was experiencing. We talked openly about the fear and how it had grown. We used simple but powerful visualisation techniques to help him reconnect with a sense of safety and control. And then, I guided him into a deep, relaxing hypnosis session – one where his mind could process things in a new, healthier way, without fear leading the conversation.

At the end of the session, he sat up, took a breath, and said something I hear quite often in these cases: 'I feel... different'.

It wasn't dramatic. But it was certain. A subtle shift had taken place.

From that day on, Daniel felt calm around food again. He went to his girlfriend's house for dinner, and not only did he manage the evening with ease – he actually enjoyed it. The fear had quietened. He felt back in control. And no, he never ate sushi again. But that was never the point.

Breakthroughs don't always happen in one session, but with the right approach – especially one that addresses both the sensory system and stored emotional memories – progress can often come sooner than most of us believe is possible.

A gentle thought to take with you:
When a child's fear shows up around food – or anything else – it's rarely about logic. It's about safety. Their world has shifted, and they need time and reassurance to feel steady again. Rather than pushing them to confront the fear head-on, the greatest gift we can offer is calm understanding. When children feel truly safe, their confidence returns – often more quickly than we expect.

READ MORE: My book *'First Aid for your Child's Mind'* has more advice for helping children overcome anxiety. Visit www.aliciaeaton. co.uk for more details.

10

WHEN HUNGER ISN'T ABOUT FOOD

Understanding your child's cravings and requests for more food.

We all know that children love treats. A biscuit after school, a fizzy drink at a party, a handful of crisps on the sofa – it's part of growing up, isn't it? But what happens when those little treats start showing up every day? When one biscuit turns into three… and somehow, they're still asking for more? You start to wonder – are they really hungry, or is something else going on?

In this chapter, we'll explore what lies beneath those constant snack requests. We'll look at the growing impact of ultra-processed foods (UPFs), how they work on your child's brain, and why they're designed to keep them coming back for more.

Most importantly, I'll show you how to tell the difference between true hunger and a craving for comfort, stimulation, or – most likely – a quick hit of dopamine. Because once you understand the psychology behind these cravings, you'll feel far more confident in guiding your child back to a calmer, more balanced relationship with food.

What a Marshmallow Can Teach Us About Healthy Habits

You may have heard of the famous **Marshmallow Test** – a psychological experiment often quoted when we talk about willpower and self-control in children. This process offers deeper lessons for us when it comes to thinking about shaping healthier eating habits for our children.

Back in the late 1960s, psychologist Walter Mischel conducted a simple yet revealing experiment at Stanford University. Preschool-aged children were each taken into a room and presented with a marshmallow on a plate. The researcher explained they could either eat it now or wait 15 minutes – and if they waited, they'd be rewarded with a second marshmallow.

Some children resisted, using every tactic they could think of – covering their eyes, singing to themselves, even turning their chairs away from the marshmallow. Others gave in almost immediately. What seemed like a fun game quickly became a fascinating window into early human behaviour.

The children were tracked for decades afterwards. Those who managed to wait tended, on average, to have better academic results, stronger social skills, and even lower levels of obesity in adulthood. It was tempting to conclude: if your child can delay gratification, they're set for life.

But more recent research has reframed this interpretation. We now understand that the ability to wait isn't just about willpower – it's about trust and life experience.

Children from more stable, consistent environments – where promises are kept and rewards are predictable – are more likely to delay gratification. After all, if your life experience has taught you that good things come when you wait, you're more likely to wait, but if your world is unpredictable, it makes perfect sense to grab what you can now.

So, what can this teach us when we're helping children build healthier eating habits?

Instead of relying solely on teaching willpower (just say no to sweets), we need to build trusting environments where healthy choices feel safe, enjoyable, and rewarding.

When children know what to expect, and see consistent routines around food and mealtimes, they're more inclined to cooperate. When adults model healthy behaviours and avoid using food as a bribe or punishment, kids learn to make thoughtful choices on their own.

In my work, I always emphasise that lasting change comes from shaping the environment first – not the child's personality. If we want them to delay the marshmallow, let's make sure they believe the second one really is coming.

Why 'just saying no' doesn't work

While it might feel tempting to clear the cupboards and say 'no more sugar', this kind of cold-turkey approach rarely works – especially with children who are already moody, irritable or craving sweets, chocolate and fast food.

A sudden removal of these foods can send their biochemistry into further chaos, triggering tantrums and emotional outbursts that test your patience to its limits. Most parents give in – understandably – and end up back where they started.

As I've said before, it by taking a closer look at the habits and routines that surround food, not the food itself – at least, not to begin with. Because it's often our daily habits, not just the ingredients we eat, that lead to excess weight, sugar dependency, and emotional eating.

Habits rarely exist in isolation – they knit together intertwined like threads in a spider's web, so tugging at one strand often causes others to shift too. That's why trying to change just one thing can feel like a battle. Instead, it's often easier – and more effective – to change several small things at the same time. Mix things up a little.

So begin with a little self-reflection. What are your own habits like? Do you regularly skip breakfast? Rely on caffeine to get through the day? Struggle with mid-afternoon cravings? If your own system is out of balance, you'll find it harder to lead your children through their own reset.

We are, by nature, creatures of habit. You may not even notice how patterned your life has become – holidaying in the same places, buying the same brands, driving the same routes. Even something as simple as your choice of tea can highlight this. With over 180 varieties on the supermarket shelf – round, square, loose-leaf, organic, herbal – most of us still grab the same box each time. Not necessarily because it tastes better, but because it's familiar. Often, it's the brand we grew up with.

And if your habits are set, chances are your children's are too. That's why I always recommend detoxing the habits first – before tackling the food.

Here are a few ideas of how you could start to mix things up a little:

- Add before you take away – introduce better foods in first, then slowly reduce the unhelpful ones.
- Change the brands – stick with the same food but try a different brand or packaging.
- Shop somewhere new – if the kids always pester you in your usual supermarket, try a different one. Walk to a local shop or visit a market instead.
- Rearrange the seating – try swapping seats around the table and see how that changes mealtime dynamics.
- Move the furniture – if your child snacks on the sofa while watching TV, simply rearranging the space can help break that association.
- Change your tableware – use different plates or smaller bowls. New colours, patterns or even sizes can alter how much food is eaten and help reset expectations.
- Change how snacks are served – a plate at the table vs. straight from the packet.
- Bring meals forward – an earlier dinner means fewer 'I need a snack' protests.
- Vary your meals – if Mondays are always Shepherd's Pie and Wednesdays always pizza, start mixing things up. Break the routine.
- Eat in new places – try a picnic: food tastes different outdoors.

Ultra-Processed Foods: Why We Keep Coming Back for More

Ultra-processed foods (UPFs) are regularly mentioned in the news nowadays and with good reason. The brightly packaged snacks, cereals, ready meals and drinks that make life easier may look very much like the snacks we all had in our own childhood, but over the years, they've changed.

These foods are made in factories not kitchens with ingredients like refined starches, cheap oils, sugars, flavourings, emulsifiers and preservatives. They've been carefully engineered by food scientists to hit the perfect balance of taste and texture. But the problem is: they're not just convenient – they're designed to be addictive. They're foods that trick the brain. The crunch of crisps, the melt-in-the-mouth feel of chocolate, the satisfying slurp of a milkshake – none of it is accidental. These experiences are built to light up your brain's reward system.

And children are especially vulnerable. Their developing brains are still learning how to regulate impulses and make decisions. So when UPFs offer a quick hit of pleasure, it's no wonder they become a go-to source of comfort, excitement, or even distraction.

Over time, regular consumption of ultra-processed foods rewires the brain's reward system. The more you eat, the more you crave. And the natural satisfaction we used to get from whole foods starts to dull. That's the real danger.

Are We Raising a Generation of Dopamine-Addicted Children?

Have you noticed how often children say, 'I'm hungry' when in all probability, they're not? Or ask for a snack minutes after finishing a meal? What we're beginning to realise now is that isn't just fussiness, boredom or habit. What's happening is deeper than that. And it's got everything to do with dopamine.

Dopamine is a powerful brain chemical. It's released whenever we experience something pleasurable – laughter, connection, praise, winning a game... or eating something delicious. It's not a bad thing. In fact, it's essential – it helps us feel motivated, focused, and rewarded. But the modern world has hijacked this system.

Ultra-processed foods are designed to send dopamine levels soaring. Salt, sugar and fat in just the right combination make the brain light up. And that's what makes them so hard to resist. Each time your child eats that snack, the brain registers it as a reward. And the brain – quite helpfully – says, 'That felt good. Let's do that again.' So the child asks for more. And more. Not necessarily because they're hungry – but because their brain has learned that food equals pleasure.

Children aren't born asking for chocolate buttons or crisps. They're born with an in-built ability to recognise hunger and fullness. But over time, that natural system can get overridden by external cues – not just from food, but from stimulation.

Children growing up in today's digital world are exposed to dopamine-triggering experiences all the time – fast-paced cartoons, bite-sized TikToks, video games, flashy ads. All of these release a quick hit of pleasure. But they also reduce their ability to sit still, focus – or feel satisfied.

The more stimulation their brain receives, the more it craves. The more it craves, the less they can tolerate boredom, quiet… or the natural pauses between meals. So they begin looking for that hit – in food. And when the brain is wired for quick rewards, snacking becomes emotional, not nutritional.

Is It Really an Addiction?

The word 'addiction' might feel strong, especially when we're talking about food. But research is increasingly supporting this idea. A major global study in 2023 found that around 12% of children show signs of dependency on ultra-processed foods – including cravings, lack of control, and even withdrawal-like symptoms when trying to cut back.

There's now even a child and adolescent version of the Yale Food Addiction Scale (YFAS) designed to track compulsive eating behaviours in young people.

Understanding What You're Really Feeling

Getting in touch with your real feelings – and learning to name them – isn't always easy. Let's face it, even we adults can struggle to tell the difference between boredom, tiredness, and true hunger. So it's a big ask to expect children to figure it out on their own.

That's why I created this **Feelings Menu** – a gentle way to help your child pause and check in with what their body and mind might really need before reaching for a snack.

Instead of asking, 'Are you sure you're hungry?' (which can feel a bit accusatory), you might say something like: *'Hmm, it's not long since lunch – let's take a look at the 'Feelings Menu' and see what your body might be trying to tell us.'*

It's not about denying them food or creating guilt – it's about building awareness. Helping your child notice whether they're thirsty, bored, tired, or simply in need of a cuddle, gives them tools they'll use for life.

You can **download a printable copy** from my website and pop it on the fridge or anywhere else handy. Use it often – make it part of your family rhythm – and over time, your child will naturally begin to tune in to their feelings and recognise what true hunger feels like.

Visit website www.aliciaeaton.co.uk for your **Feelings Menu**

Feelings Menu

Hungry

My tummy's rumbling:
I definitely need
some food.

Thirsty

My mouth feels dry:
I think I need a drink.

Bored

I've got nothing to do:
I need to be busy.

Ignored

Everyone is busy:
I feel lonely and need
to talk to someone.

Tired

I've been up for hours:
I need to have a rest.

Sad

I'm upset and feel
like crying: I need a hug.

Angry

I'm feeling annoyed:
I need something to
help me relax.

Restless

I've been sitting down
all day: I need to run
around.

IN THE THERAPY ROOM

Grief, Guilt, and the Need for Goodbye

Isabella aged 21, came to see me because she felt something was beginning to spiral out of control. Over the last few weeks, she'd developed a pattern of binge-eating – microwave meals, bars of chocolate, cakes, anything quick and sugary. She would eat until she felt sick – and then sit with the wave of shame that followed. She told me, quite plainly, 'I don't want this to turn into something serious. I can feel where this is going'.

She could already sense that this behaviour wasn't about the food – it was about something deeper. And as we talked, the real story began to unfold.

A few weeks earlier, Isabella's grandmother had passed away. She explained that her grandmother had been in a hospice for some time, and the family had known the end was near. On a Saturday morning, just before lunchtime, she received a phone call from her sister. Their mother was already at the hospice, and her grandmother had suddenly taken a turn. Isabella was told that she needed to come – quickly.

Isabella hesitated. She hadn't eaten lunch yet and thought it best to do so before going. She made herself toasted cheese sandwiches, slowly, methodically. She had a cup of coffee. Then a slice of cake. It became, in her words, 'a long, heavy lunch'. She'd dragged her heels.

By the time she arrived at the hospice, it was too late. Her grandmother had died just moments before.

As Isabella recounted this to me, I could feel the pain she was carrying. It wasn't just sadness – it was guilt. She hadn't missed her grandmother's final moment because of traffic or a delayed train. She believed she'd missed it because she chose to eat instead.

In that moment, her binge-eating started to make sense. She wasn't eating for comfort – she was punishing herself.

In our session, I guided her gently into a deep state of hypnosis. Together, we went back to that pivotal moment – the one where she received the phone call. But this time, we rewrote the ending. In her mind's eye, she saw herself arriving in time, walking into her grandmother's room. She imagined being able to say the things she had needed to say, to hold her grandmother's hand, to give the apology she felt she owed. It was emotional and powerful.

When the session ended, Isabella sat quietly for a while, then said, 'It feels like I was there. Like she heard me.' And perhaps, in some way, she had. Because as Isabella explained later, she still felt her grandmother's presence around her. And now, the guilt had lifted – she felt very strongly that her grandmother would not want her to continue punishing herself with food. Her eating patterns calmed, naturally and gently – not because I told her what to eat, but because she no longer needed food as a form of self-reproach.

Sometimes, the work isn't about food at all. It's about permission. Forgiveness. And finding peace with the moments we wish had gone differently.

A gentle thought to take with you:

Whether it's a child reaching for biscuits or an adult standing in front of the fridge, these moments aren't always about hunger. More often, they're quiet signals – of sadness, stress, or something unresolved. When we learn to pause and ask, 'What is it I really need right now?', the answer is rarely food. It's comfort, clarity, connection. And once we understand that, we can begin to make different choices – for ourselves, and for those we care about.

READ MORE: Check out my book *'Words that Work: How to Get Kids to Do Almost Anything'* for more ideas on how to say 'no' to snacks without actually using that word.

11

WHEN YOUR CHILD IS OVERWEIGHT: WHAT YOU CAN DO

Why We Can't Always See What's Right in Front of Us

It's one of the hardest things to admit – but often, we simply don't see what others see. Especially when it comes to our children.

If someone were to ask you whether your child is overweight, you might say no – and truly believe it. Not because you're ignoring the truth or being careless, but because your love for your child naturally clouds your vision. And you're not alone.

A major research review published in the *International Journal of Obesity* found that nearly half of all parents underestimate their child's weight – with many describing overweight or even obese children as having a 'normal' body shape. This isn't neglect. It's a deeply human response.

When something becomes more common – like larger bodies – it starts to look more normal. And when all the children in the playground start to look a little rounder, it's easy to think, 'They all look the same – nothing to worry about.'

But there's something else at work here, too: a kind of protective filter. As parents, we are biologically wired to love and defend our children. We want to protect them from harm – including hurtful labels or judgments. So it makes perfect sense that we might struggle to see something that feels painful, shameful, or even like a reflection on us.

If you're reading this and recognising some of those feelings – guilt, defensiveness, worry – please don't be hard on yourself. This isn't about blame. It's about awareness.

And once we become aware, we can begin to make small, powerful changes – all it takes is a bit more knowledge, a better understanding of how habits are formed, and the confidence to guide our children through it.

Why Age Six Matters More Than We Thought

There's now mounting evidence to suggest that the age of six is a critical tipping point in a child's weight journey. At the 2025 *European Congress on Obesity*, Dutch researchers shared a study showing that children who are overweight at six are highly likely to carry that weight into their teens and beyond. In other words: if we want to change the outcome for our children, we need to start earlier than we think. Not with diets or restriction – but with simple habits, made at home, that gently support balance and health from the beginning.

A 2025 report by the *Lancet Commission on Adolescent Health and Wellbeing* warns that by 2030, 464 million adolescents worldwide will be living with obesity or overweight, marking a significant increase since 2015. Studies have found that increased consumption of ultra-processed foods (UPFs) among young people is associated with elevated food addiction and negative mood scores.

These findings highlight the critical role that today's teenagers and young adults play in shaping healthier food environments for future generations.

Because let's be honest – the implications of growing up overweight go far beyond the number on the scales. These children aren't just carrying extra kilos – they're often carrying a heavier emotional load too. Low self-esteem, fewer friendships, avoidance of sports or group activities, even being left out socially – these experiences shape how a child sees themselves, and the world around them. And that sense of 'not fitting in' doesn't always vanish with age. It can quietly follow them into adolescence and adulthood.

By the time they reach adulthood, the pattern may be even more entrenched. Studies have shown that adults who grew up overweight are more likely to face discrimination in the workplace – whether in hiring, promotion, or salary. This, in turn, affects financial independence, mental wellbeing, and overall life satisfaction. And while the media often focuses on appearance or clothing size, the real story is deeper – about confidence, opportunity, and feeling comfortable in your own skin.

But this doesn't mean we need to panic. Far from it. What it does mean is that the earlier we notice unhelpful patterns – oversized portions, food used for comfort, or a reliance on ultra-processed snacks – then the more time we have to gently nudge things in a better direction. Children's bodies are still growing. Their habits are still forming. And with the right support, they can – and do – change course. One calm conversation, one smaller portion, one new routine at a time.

Misconceptions About Childhood Obesity and Socioeconomic Status

It's easy to assume that childhood obesity is a problem linked only to lower income backgrounds – and it's true that children from less affluent households are statistically more likely to struggle with weight. Factors like access to fresh food, safe places to play, and reliable routines all make a difference. But that's only part of the story.

Obesity is now a challenge facing families right across the socio-economic spectrum. In middle – and high-income households – children may have access to an abundance of food, especially the ultra-processed kind, along with digital devices, long hours of screen time, and fewer spontaneous opportunities for active play. Busy schedules often mean an increased reliance on takeaways and restaurant meals becoming a part of everyday life, rather than an occasional treat.

Meanwhile, there are many lower-income families who manage to serve home-cooked meals, encourage physical activity, and maintain strong routines – reminding us that financial status isn't the only factor in a child's health.

Ultimately, it's not about income alone. Tackling childhood obesity means looking at the full picture – not just the bank balance.

Childhood Obesity: How France Compares to the UK and US

Across Europe and beyond, childhood obesity has become one of the most pressing health concerns of our time. But when we compare countries like France, the UK, and the US, we begin to see some striking differences.

According to the World Health Organization (2024), France reports some of the lowest childhood obesity rates in Europe, with just 8.2% of children aged 5–19 classified as obese. For younger children aged 7–9, the rate is around 11% – still significantly below that of other nations.

In contrast, the UK has one of the highest rates in Europe. According to NHS Digital (2022–23), 22.7% of children aged 10–11 are classified as obese, and over one third (37.6%) are overweight or obese by the end of primary school. These figures mark a sharp increase from earlier ages.

Meanwhile, the US records the highest average national obesity rate among children, with 19.7% of children aged 2–19 classified as obese, according to the CDC. The numbers climb further depending on age and location, with some states reporting rates exceeding 26%.

What makes these figures especially important is that French children aren't eating radically different foods – their diets still include bread, cheese, and sweet treats. The difference lies in the 'how and when'. Structure, routine, and a cultural mindset toward food play a key role.

France enjoys one of the lowest childhood obesity rates in the developed world – not because of restriction, dieting, or fear, but because of cultural habits that support mindful, structured eating.

What French Families Do Differently

1. Meals Have Structure and Rhythm

French children typically eat three meals a day and one set snack time – often around 4pm (called le goûter). That's it. No constant grazing. No snack drawer to dip into whenever they feel bored. This rhythm helps children tune into real hunger and naturally regulates their appetite.

2. Eating Happens at the Table

Whether it's breakfast, lunch, or dinner, meals are eaten sitting down – and ideally, together. Even in school canteens, lunch is served in multiple courses with proper cutlery and no rush. This reinforces that food is something to be enjoyed and respected – not something to eat mindlessly while walking, watching, or scrolling.

3. Snacking Is Rare – and Treated Differently

Snacks aren't handed out automatically in the car or in front of the TV. They're treated more like mini-meals, served on a plate, with real food. A piece of baguette, a square of dark chocolate, some fruit. Children learn to wait for meals and they learn that it's okay to feel hungry between them – experiencing feelings of hunger, means you'll enjoy the next meal, all the more.

4. Food Isn't Used to Manage Behaviour

French parents rarely bribe children with sweets, reward them with pudding, or soothe their tears with chocolate. They separate food from feelings – so children don't learn to eat for comfort, distraction, or emotional regulation. Instead, feelings are acknowledged and addressed in other ways – a cuddle, a talk, a walk, or simply sitting with discomfort.

5. Portion Sizes Are Smaller – But More Satisfying

In France, children are served smaller portions of richer food – and they're encouraged to eat slowly, savour each bite, and stop when they've had enough. Pleasure comes from quality, not quantity. Food is flavourful, well-prepared, and rarely rushed.

6. There's Less Guilt, More Trust

Perhaps most importantly, there's a sense of calm around food. French parents don't moralise eating – food isn't 'naughty' or 'bad'. It's not something to feel guilty about or obsess over. Instead, there's trust

– trust that children can learn to enjoy food in a balanced way, that their bodies know when they've had enough, and that structure, not control, is what keeps things on track.

These practices don't require a different postcode or perfect parenting. They just require a shift in mindset – one that says: we don't need to fix food, we just need to relate to it differently.

Are You Feeding Your Child Too Much?

It's not always easy to tell. We're surrounded by big portions, oversized plates, and constant snacking – and before long, it becomes hard to spot what's 'normal' anymore. Here are a few quiet clues that might help you tune in:

Take a look at portion sizes.
If your child's serving is similar to your own – or plated on the same size dish – chances are, it's too much. Children's stomachs are far smaller than adults', and many of today's dinner plates are significantly larger than they used to be. A smaller plate might be a good starting point.

Watch out for the fairness trap.
Do you find yourself dishing up identical portions 'to keep things fair'? I remember a time when my children began counting the chips on their plates to check they'd been treated equally. My five-year-old daughter had fewer than her ten-year-old brother – which, of course, was intentional. I explained that fairness isn't about giving everyone the same – it's about giving each child what's right for them.

Could your 'picky eater' simply be full?
If your child isn't hungry for their next meal, it might not be fussy eating at all. It could be that they've simply had too much earlier in

the day. Snacks have become far more frequent than they used to be – once a day has crept up to two or three, often without us noticing.

Do they always have to finish what's on their plate?
Encouraging children to 'clear their plate' might seem like a good habit – but it can actually teach them to override their natural hunger cues. If we don't listen to our body when it says 'I've had enough', we risk losing touch with that signal altogether.

Check how clothes are fitting.
Tightness around the chest, waist, or bottom – even when your child hasn't grown taller – can be a gentle early indicator that intake is outpacing growth. Don't panic. Sometimes a growth spurt is just around the corner. But if you're noticing it consistently, it may be time to take a closer look at what's going on.

Are snacks becoming automatic?
If your child gets a snack the moment they walk through the door, before checking whether they're actually hungry – it might be more of a habit than a need. Try a simple pause: 'Let's have a glass of water and see how you feel in a few minutes'. Often, the request passes.

Does your child eat while distracted?
Eating in front of a screen – whether it's the TV, tablet or phone – can override your child's ability to notice when they're full. Meals and snacks eaten mindfully, at a table, help children connect with the act of eating and better understand their own signals.

Are food choices driven by mood, not hunger?
If your child asks for food when they're bored, tired, upset, or seeking comfort, it's worth pausing. Gently help them connect with what they're really feeling. This is where tools like the 'Feelings Menu' in the earlier chapter can be invaluable.

Do you finish their leftovers for them?

This one's more for the grown-ups! Many parents nibble from their child's plate out of habit – not hunger – and it makes it harder to demonstrate mindful eating, especially if it's done standing up or walking towards the dishwasher. It's important for us to model good behaviour, so treat the food on your child's plate as theirs, even if it goes unfinished. You'll be doing yourself a favour too!

When Is Food Not Really Food?

Many of the families I work with tell me they cook healthy meals, don't allow endless treats, and aren't fans of fast food so they can't understand why they've put on weight. I tell them it's because calories aren't just coming from mealtimes anymore. They're quietly woven into everyday moments – often without us noticing.

That's why I like to ask: When is a food not really a food? Let's take a look.

1. When It's a Toy

The lines between food and play are getting blurrier. A bracelet you can eat? A chocolate egg with a toy inside? Ham printed with smiley faces? When food becomes entertainment, we stop recognising it as fuel. It becomes something else entirely – a game, a treat, a distraction. And because play is often frequent, so is the food that comes with it. Try to keep food and play separate. It might seem harmless, but it teaches children that eating is part of the fun, not just something we do to nourish the body.

2. When It's a Gift

We celebrate everything these days – and usually with food. Chocolate boxes, cakes, sweet hampers, giant cookies… They've become the default gift for birthdays, thank-you's, anniversaries, and end-of-term celebrations. Now, children (and adults) are surrounded by edible gifts year-round. This normalises excess and makes it harder to see food as a physical need, rather than an emotional gesture. When giving or receiving gifts, consider alternatives: books, candles, bath treats, crafts, flowers. Let's show our children that not every celebration has to come with sugar.

3. When It's a Reward

We all love a treat. But when food is used to reward effort – especially sugary snacks – it teaches the brain to link success with sweetness. It starts with star charts and stickers. One good deed, one chocolate button. But over time, this can wire the mind to expect food as a payoff. That's not helpful when we want our children to develop inner motivation – doing the right thing because it's right, not for the biscuit at the end of it.

Allow treats now and again, but try not to link them to behaviour. Let them stay as part of balanced enjoyment, not part of a transaction.

4. When It's a Celebration

Food and celebration have always gone hand in hand – birthday cakes, festive feasts, Sunday roasts. And that's okay. But something has shifted. Celebrations have multiplied, and with them, the food. Where once parties were occasional and simple, now there are party bags, themed cupcakes, dessert tables, and an event every weekend. We're not just marking birthdays – we're celebrating half-terms, end-of-school weeks, lost teeth, even playdates. And each one often comes with another sugar rush.

We can still create joy and excitement – just without the constant snacks. Treasure hunts, dance parties, homemade decorations, picnics in the garden… These are what memories are made of. Let food be part of the fun – but not the whole event.

5. When It's a Commiseration

A scraped knee. A rough day. A moment of tears. It's so easy to reach for the biscuit tin and offer something sweet to cheer them up – and who could blame us? It works, after all… at least for a moment. But over time, this sends a powerful message: uncomfortable feelings can be soothed with food. It's how emotional eating begins. Not because of greed or indulgence, but because a child learns that sadness, frustration or anxiety = sugar.

There are other ways to offer comfort. A cuddle. A warm bath. Drawing together. Sitting with them and simply saying, 'That was hard'. These create real emotional safety – without the calories.

So, what can we take from all this?

Now you can begin to see just how easily extra, unnecessary calories slip into our lives – not during meals, but in all the little moments in between. A treat here, a reward there, a celebration, a commiseration… It all adds up. Think back to the earlier chapter where I described the Compound Effect.

But here's the good news: these are the easiest calories to remove. They're not part of proper meals, they don't nourish – and they're often not even noticed. That's where change can begin. Not with a dramatic diet overhaul, but with a quiet awareness of what food is really for – and where it truly belongs.

The Subtle Harm of Weight Talk: Why Our Words Matter More Than We Think

As parents, we want to guide our children towards a healthy, happy life. We help them brush their teeth, wear seatbelts, and eat their vegetables. But when it comes to conversations around food and weight, even well-intended words can leave deep, lasting impressions.

Children are always listening – absorbing not just what we say, but how we feel about ourselves and our bodies. This is why the language we use around food, weight, and appearance matters more than we might realise.

It can be tempting to believe that drawing attention to our child's eating habits or body shape will help them make better choices. But research consistently shows that focusing on weight can actually fuel the very behaviours we're trying to prevent. Children who are frequently reminded about food or size may start to:

- Feel guilt or shame around eating – Calling certain foods 'bad' can make children feel bad for simply enjoying them.
- Hide their eating – Strict rules or pressure often push children to eat in secret, leading to disordered habits.
- Struggle with self-worth – Comparisons to siblings or comments like 'You need to be careful' can damage a child's confidence and body image.

Even casual remarks can echo for years. A single comment might seem small to us, but to a young mind, it can become a fixed belief.

Should You Say Anything If They Haven't Noticed?

This brings us to a question many parents quietly wrestle with: Should I bring it up? Do I need to say something?

If your child appears to be gaining weight but hasn't mentioned it themselves, the kindest and most effective path may be the quieter one. Research from the University of Bath suggests that open, thoughtful conversations can help build trust – but only when the child is already expressing concern. Otherwise, introducing the idea of a 'weight problem' too soon can do more harm than good.

The American Academy of Paediatrics echoes this, encouraging parents to focus on creating a healthy environment – not delivering messages about body shape. That means modelling calm, consistent habits: family meals, plenty of movement, good sleep, and balanced routines.

Children learn by what they see, not just what they hear. You don't need to point out what's 'wrong' – just begin modelling what's right.

But what if your child brings it up first?

Sometimes, despite your best efforts to create a calm, body-positive environment, your child may come to you with worries of their own. They might have been teased at school, seen something online, or simply noticed that their body feels different from their friends.

When that moment arrives – often quietly, sometimes tearfully – it's important to respond in a way that reassures rather than alarms. This is your chance to offer support, not solutions; to focus on feelings, not fixes. And most importantly, to remind them that they are loved, just as they are, while helping them move forward with confidence.

How to Talk to Your Child About Weight – With Sensitivity and Support

When a child expresses worries about their weight, it's tempting to rush in with reassurance or solutions. But the most powerful thing you can offer, first and foremost, is calm presence and quiet confidence. Your child needs to feel safe, heard, and accepted – not fixed.

Instead of rushing to correct or downplay their feelings, try gently acknowledging them:

- *Thank you for telling me that – it takes courage to talk about things like this.*
- *You're not alone in this. We can figure it out together.*
- *Your body is growing and changing all the time and we'll support it in doing that the best way we can.*

The goal isn't to focus on the weight itself, but to guide your child toward habits that help them feel good – emotionally, physically, and mentally.

Small Shifts That Make a Big Difference

Here are ways to help your child feel more confident and in control of their health, without ever turning it into a 'diet':

Focus on what you can add, not what you take away.
Encourage colour, texture, and variety on the plate. Think:

- A handful of berries added to breakfast
- A plate of crunchy veggie sticks before dinner
- Chilled water and fruit as the default after-school option

Say something like:

- Let's see how many colours we can eat today – red, orange, green…

Be mindful of the words you use.

- Children are attuned not just to what we say – but how we talk about ourselves. Avoid phrases like:

- *You shouldn't be eating that.*
- *I feel so fat today.*

Instead, shift the focus to how food supports the body:
- *Let's choose something that helps us feel strong and full of energy.*
- *Your body works hard for you – food gives it the fuel it needs.*

Movement should feel like fun, not punishment.
Activity doesn't need to be formal or timed. It can be joyful and spontaneous:
- Dancing in the living room
- Racing to the post box
- Playing a silly game outside

You might say:
- *Let's see if we can beat our steps from yesterday!*
- *Shall we see if we can invent a new dance move?*

Build their confidence from the inside out.
Remind your child that who they are goes far beyond how they look. Talk about:
- Their kindness, creativity, humour
- What they're good at – even something simple, such as looking after a pet
- What they love doing
- How their body is just one part of them – but it's not the whole story.

Shape the environment – not the conversation.
Rather than making changes about them, let it be a quiet, family-wide shift:
- Keep healthier foods visible and within reach
- Swap fizzy drinks for water
- Wind down with calming bedtime routines

And finally... watch gently.

If your child is withdrawing, skipping meals, or hiding their eating, they may need more support than you can give alone. In these cases, speak to a GP, therapist, or school counsellor experienced in children's mental and emotional health. Sometimes, the most healing words are the simplest:

- *I love you exactly as you are.*
- *We're in this together.*
- *You're growing, changing, and that's a wonderful thing.*

Why Your Child's Tummy Might Be Telling You They're Stressed

It's often said that children today are gaining weight simply because they're not moving enough. We imagine them sitting for hours on end, eyes glued to screens, thumbs twitching on controllers – and conclude that it's all about lack of exercise. But what if the real culprit isn't just the stillness, but the stress?

Recent scientific research is showing us something rather surprising: it's not just the sitting that matters, but what your child is doing while they're sitting. Studies have found that elevated levels of cortisol – that's the hormone we produce in response to stress – are closely linked to the build-up of fat around the tummy area in children. This kind of fat, known as visceral fat, isn't just an aesthetic concern. It's also associated with greater risks for metabolic and cardiovascular issues later in life.

In fact, one study published in the journal Psychoneuroendocrinology found that children who experienced higher cortisol levels in the mornings and in response to school-related stress were more likely to carry fat around their middles. Another large-scale review confirmed this, showing that long-term exposure to high cortisol (measured in hair samples) was linked to increased fat and body mass in kids.

So, what does this mean for us as parents?

Well, here's where it gets interesting. We often assume that video games are harmful purely because they encourage our children to sit still. But let's think back for a moment. In the 70s, 80s, and even early 90s, not every child was leaping around the garden or cycling through the woods. Many spent plenty of time indoors too – sitting, reading books, doodling, watching TV or building Lego. They were sedentary, yes, but not stressed. Today's screen time is different.

Computer games, especially the fast-paced or violent ones, are deliberately designed to keep children on high alert. They flood the system with adrenaline, activating the body's fight or flight mode – and with that comes a surge in cortisol. Even when the child looks relaxed on the outside, internally, their system is being pumped with stress chemicals.

And here's the twist: that stress may be telling your child's body to hold on to fat, particularly around the tummy. The body, interpreting the stress as danger, prepares for survival. And one way it does this is by stockpiling energy – in the form of abdominal fat.

So yes, sitting still matters. But what matters even more is what your child is doing while they're sitting still. A quiet hour of colouring, listening to music, reading, or watching a gentle TV show is very different from an hour of high-octane, adrenaline-charged gaming.

This doesn't mean you need to ban all computer games – it's not about extremes. But it's worth creating balance. Offer plenty of opportunities for your child to unwind in calm, grounding ways. Reading, drawing, imaginative play – all can soothe the nervous system and help lower cortisol levels.

In the end, the key isn't just moving more – it's feeling safe, secure, and calm. Helping your child find that emotional balance might just be one of the best things you can do for their physical health.

Why Sleep Matters More Than You Think

When we think about childhood obesity, it's easy to focus solely on food – what children are eating, how much, and how often. But one often overlooked factor that can quietly fuel weight gain is something far less obvious: sleep. Or rather, the lack of it.

We now know that children who aren't getting enough good-quality sleep are more likely to crave sugary, high-calorie foods the next day. It's not just a matter of tiredness making them grumpy or irritable – there's something far deeper going on.

Sleep directly affects two key hormones that regulate appetite: ghrelin and leptin. When children are sleep-deprived, ghrelin (the hormone that makes us feel hungry) increases, while leptin (the one that signals fullness) decreases.

The result? Their brain starts encouraging them to seek out quick energy fixes – often in the form of biscuits, crisps, or anything sweet and fast. This isn't about poor willpower – it's biology doing its' job. A tired brain is simply more likely to demand easy energy.

But as parents, we can offer guidance by looking not just at what's on the plate, but what's happening in the bedtime routine too. Is your child getting enough rest? Are screens and stimulation creeping too close to sleep time? Making even small changes to improve your child's sleep can often have a surprising ripple effect – calmer moods, fewer cravings, and more balanced eating during the day.

Helping children build healthy habits around food starts with supporting their overall wellbeing. Sleep, movement, calm routines – it's all connected. So before you start changing what's in the lunchbox, it's worth pausing to ask: is my child simply tired and reaching for comfort?

Recommended Sleep Durations by Age:

Age Group	Recommended Sleep Duration
4–12 months	12–16 hours (including naps)
1–2 years	11–14 hours (including naps)
3–5 years	10–13 hours (including naps)
6–12 years	9–12 hours
13–18 years	8–10 hours

These guidelines are endorsed by the American Academy of Paediatrics and the American Academy of Sleep Medicine. They are based on research linking adequate sleep to improved attention, behavior, learning, memory, emotional regulation, and overall mental and physical health.

The NHS also provides similar recommendations, emphasizing the importance of sufficient sleep for children's development and well-being.

What I Hope You'll Take Away

You don't need to overhaul your child's diet overnight. You don't need to turn into a nutritionist or a personal trainer. What really matters is consistency – and staying calm.

By gently reshaping routines, creating a home where healthy habits feel normal, and responding with confidence rather than fear, you'll start to see changes. Not just on the outside, but in the way your child feels inside. With small, steady steps over the months and years ahead, you'll be helping them build a lifelong foundation – one that leads to strength, balance, and self-belief. And that's worth every effort.

IN THE THERAPY ROOM

When the Craving Isn't Really for Sugar

Dorcas was just 12 when she came to see me. Quiet, wide-eyed, and carrying far more than a child her age should. Her mother had brought her in with a very specific concern: she believed her daughter was overweight and eating too many sweet things – biscuits, sweets, and treats after school. 'She's craving sugar constantly', her mother told me, 'and I want you to help her stop'.

She was stern about it, too – adamant that there would be no new clothes for Dorcas until she lost some weight. And sure enough, when I met her, I could see the trousers that didn't quite reach her ankles anymore. She'd outgrown them, but they weren't going to be replaced.

At first glance, it might have seemed like the focus should be on Dorcas – helping her break the habit of buying sweets or reaching for biscuits. But as we talked, it became clear that this wasn't the real problem. Not really.

What began to emerge was something deeper. Dorcas's parents had recently divorced. The emotional landscape of her home had shifted, and with it, so had the dynamic between her and her mother. Her mum wasn't just worried about her daughter's weight. She was also – perhaps more urgently – worried about her own.

In our sessions, she admitted fears that she might be single forever, that no one would find her attractive again, that she had somehow 'lost herself'. And in that moment of personal uncertainty, her daughter's changing body had become the lightning rod for all her fear.

It was Dorcas, not her mum, who absorbed the tension. She was the one being told she needed to change. But it wasn't her who needed help. So I shifted the focus of the work.

I began seeing Dorcas's mother separately. We talked, not about sugar or calories, but about fear and what it means to move forward after heartbreak. I helped her find her confidence again, to feel more secure in herself and less defined by the mirror – or by the worry of what others might think.

As the mother became calmer and more confident, the need for control over Dorcas began to soften. The sharp edges of her language began to blur. She stopped threatening, stopped monitoring every bite. The pressure at home lifted.

And Dorcas? She began to settle too.

Her cravings started to subside. The biscuits weren't as important anymore. She seemed to relax into herself again – no longer eating in rebellion or secrecy. The dynamic had changed, and so had the need for the coping mechanism.

I gently reminded her mother of something she had forgotten: that nature was on their side. At 12, Dorcas was on the brink of a growth spurt. Her body would stretch and shift and evolve, as children's bodies are meant to do. With the pressure removed, she would soon begin to look slimmer naturally – not because she was 'fixed', but because she was growing. The real change wasn't about food. It was about emotional safety. For both of them.

A gentle thought to take with you

Next time your child seems to be craving something sweet, pause and ask yourself: What else might they be hungry for right now? Comfort, attention, reassurance? Often, when we meet the emotional need, the need for food fades on its own.

12

BODY IMAGE – GROWING UP IN THE SPOTLIGHT

Society's Obsession with Thinness

In the past, a child's view of their body was shaped by a relatively small circle – siblings, friends at school, perhaps a celebrity glimpsed occasionally on television. But today's children are growing up in a very different world, one where comparison is not only constant but global.

Thanks to social media, they're exposed to an endless stream of influencers, celebrities, and wellness experts – all sharing carefully curated versions of themselves. And while much of this content appears positive on the surface, the underlying message is often the same: to be accepted, you must look a certain way.

The wellness industry has grown rapidly in recent years, now worth billions. And while many of its voices speak in the language of self-care and empowerment, the truth is that much of this messaging depends on making people feel that they're somehow not quite enough.

You're not slim enough, not calm enough, not fit enough – but you could be, if only you bought this product or followed that plan. For children and teenagers, still learning who they are, this can quietly chip away at their self-esteem.

On top of that, we're seeing the emotional impact of online bullying – often focused, unsurprisingly, on appearance. A cruel comment made in the playground might once have been forgotten within a few days. But now, it's written down, recorded, even shared. It's no longer a private moment – it's on display, often for the entire school community to see. That kind of scrutiny stays with a child, and it hurts.

So, it's no surprise that many young people today are struggling to feel at ease in their own skin. When they're constantly surrounded by messages telling them how they should look, and their appearance becomes a target for judgement or ridicule, it's easy to see how this begins to affect their confidence – and their mental health.

And when a child feels uncomfortable in their own skin, it can begin to affect how they relate to food. Some may restrict their eating to lose weight or gain control, while others may turn to food for comfort when emotions become overwhelming.

That's why it's so important we help our children navigate these pressures with understanding and calm. When we take the time to listen and support them, we create space for a healthier relationship with both their bodies and food.

When the Hurt Comes Through a Screen: Helping Your Child After Online Body Shaming

It's the moment every parent dreads – your child, tearful and withdrawn, shows you a cruel comment or an unkind photo shared online. Maybe someone has mocked their weight or ridiculed their appearance. And now, the confident, happy child you know so well seems to be shrinking in front of your eyes, suddenly unsure of their worth.

As heartbreaking as this moment is, it's also an opportunity – an opportunity to remind your child that their value was never measured in likes, comments, or clothing size. And a chance to help them build a quiet inner confidence that no bully can take away.

1. Start With Safety and Reassurance

Your calm presence is the most powerful thing you can offer right now. Before rushing to problem-solve, just be there. Sit beside them, listen without judgment, and let them feel your support.

You might say: *'I can see this really hurt you. I'm so sorry this happened. None of it is true – and you didn't deserve it'*.

Let your voice be steady, reassuring, and full of belief in who they are. If needed, take practical steps together to restore a sense of safety:
– Block or report the accounts responsible.
– Save any evidence in case it's needed later.
– Encourage a healthy break from the screen.
– Adjust privacy settings to limit further exposure.

2. Talk About Feelings Before Fixing

It's natural to want to make it better straight away – but right now, your child's emotions need space. You could say: *'These comments say far more about the person who wrote them than they do about you. But that doesn't mean they don't hurt'*.

Help your child name what they're feeling: *'You might be feeling embarrassed, angry, confused – or even ashamed. And that's okay. Anyone would feel like that'*.

You're showing them that feeling hurt doesn't make them weak – it makes them human.

3. Protect Their Inner Belief System

Children are deeply influenced by what they hear and see, especially from peers or social media figures. Now is the time to gently remind them of what's true:

– Their body is not the problem.
– Their worth isn't up for public vote.
– No one else gets to decide how they feel about themselves.

You might say: *'Your body is yours. It carries you through your day, helps you run, laugh, and hug. It doesn't need to be smaller – or different – to be lovable'.*

4. Nurture the Roots of Self-Worth

After a knock like this, your child needs reminders – subtle, regular ones – of who they are beyond their appearance. Help them reconnect with:

– Activities they enjoy and feel competent in.
– People who make them feel safe, valued, and seen.
– Moments that spark joy, curiosity, or calm.

You might create a gentle daily ritual: *'Let's name one thing about you today that has nothing to do with how you look – something kind, clever, or brave'.* These small moments begin to rebuild their inner dialogue.

5. Talk About Social Media Like a Mirror

Explain that social media isn't reality – it's often a distorted mirror. People post from insecurity, try to impress, or act impulsively. And sometimes they forget that there's a real person on the other side of the screen.

You could say: *'Imagine those comments were scribbled on a bathroom wall. Would you believe them? Or would you see them for what they are – graffiti, not truth?'*

6. Moving Forward, Together

Cruel words can leave lasting marks – but with your support, your child can come through this stronger, more compassionate, and more resilient.

Gently remind them: *'One day, this will be just a small part of your story. But the kindness you show yourself now – that's what shapes the rest'.*

And when they're ready, you might help them explore how they can be a voice of support for others, too. Because often, healing doesn't just come from being supported – it comes from realising we're strong enough to support someone else.

Making Friends With The Mirror

Looking in the mirror is often a baby's favourite pastime – we're all naturally drawn to the human face. That fascination continues into middle childhood, when children love to pull faces, sing into hairbrushes, and dance around, completely absorbed in their own reflection. This is the happy 'look at me!' stage of life.

Then comes adolescence. With it arrive powerful psychological shifts and the unsettling feeling of being thrown into the spotlight. This isn't imagined – it's a genuine sense of being watched, as the teenager begins to develop a clearer 'sense of self'. Dressing like their peers and following fashion trends isn't just about fitting in – it's often a way to avoid standing out and becoming a target for attention.

The clumsy coordination that often comes with sudden growth spurts – explaining why teenagers might knock things over or fumble at the dinner table – only adds to the self-consciousness that's already there.

And as they grapple with these changes, they're surrounded by glossy images of perfection on social media and an ongoing cultural obsession with celebrities and size-zero ideals. This constant exposure creates a dangerous emotional cocktail. For some teenagers, dieting and shrinking into smaller clothes isn't about being healthy – it's about disappearing altogether.

Psychologists define body image as the thoughts, perceptions, and feelings we have about our bodies. So when your child looks in the mirror, they're not necessarily seeing what you see. They're seeing what they believe about themselves. Thankfully, there are practical ways to help.

I mentioned earlier in this book that I spent many years assisting Paul McKenna with his well-known Weight Loss Seminars. At a key moment during the day, we would use a powerful NLP technique designed to help people make friends with their image in the mirror. I often worked with 20 to 30 delegates individually in quick succession, using this method.

Standing in front of a full length mirror, I'd work with one person at a time and say: *'Tell me what you don't like about yourself'*. And, we'd then move on to changing those feelings. Most people started slowly, reeling off the usual list – 'my thighs, my stomach' – but very quickly, the words would turn into a torrent of self-criticism.

I was always struck by how fast people could turn on themselves. And soon the complaints would shift to things they couldn't change: *'I don't like the colour of my eyes', 'I've never liked the shape of my hands'* or *'I'm the wrong height'.*

I heard those phrases again and again. And after all those years running those seminars, I still couldn't work out what the 'right' height was meant to be.

The truth is: you are your own harshest critic. And the more you criticise yourself, the more permission you give others to do the same.

But remember: your child is watching. If they see you criticising yourself in the mirror, they'll learn to do the same. This shapes their self-image for life. That's why building self-esteem is so important. High self-esteem helps protect against body dissatisfaction.

What we actually see in the mirror is a reflection of how we feel 'on the inside' and not how we look 'on the outside'. We get a distorted, inaccurate image of ourselves.

We all know people who don't meet conventional beauty standards yet seem to breeze through job interviews, build great relationships, and command attention in a room. That's no coincidence. When you feel good on the inside, it shows on the outside.

Helping your child make friends with their reflection isn't just a feel-good exercise – it's a life skill. One that will shape their confidence, their relationships, and their future.

I've adapted the 'Mirror Exercise' we used with adults on those seminars to make it more suitable for children. I don't feel it's appropriate to ask children to list what they don't like about themselves – so here's what I suggest we do instead.

THE MAGIC MIRROR EXERCISE

Use this simple self-esteem ritual to help children feel good in their own skin.

We often teach our children to be kind to others – but what if we helped them practice being kind to themselves, too? The Magic Mirror exercise is a gentle way to help your child begin noticing what's right about them – rather than what they think needs to change. By focusing on small, positive things they see in their reflection, children begin to build a stronger, more compassionate relationship with themselves.

How to Do It

Try this exercise three to four times a week, either in the morning before school or as part of a bedtime routine. You could even practise it in your regular Family Meeting and have everyone take part. Keep it light and positive.

Stand Together

Invite your child to stand in front of a mirror. You can stand with them, or just nearby offering gentle support.

Ask Them to Notice

Say something like:

'Let's look into the mirror and find three things you like about what you see. They can be little things – maybe your smiley eyes, your strong arms, your curly hair.'

Encourage them to say each one out loud

'I like my... eyes, because they sparkle when I laugh.'
'I like my... legs, because they help me run fast.'
'I like my... hair, because it's fun to brush and style.'

Encourage the Language of Love

Gradually, move from 'I like…' to 'I love…' to deepen the sense of self-appreciation.

'I love my hands – they help me draw cool pictures'.

'I love my cheeks – they go pink when I giggle'.

This isn't about vanity – it's about value. Learning to say kind things to yourself helps shape the beliefs that stay with you for life.

Keep It Playful and Light

Let it be fun. If they're feeling shy or silly, that's okay. You might go first or make it a family tradition.

Why It Works

Just like a gratitude journal trains the brain to notice what's going well, the 'Magic Mirror Exercise' helps your child focus on what's right about themselves – not what they (or others) think they should fix. Over time, this simple practice can:

– Boost confidence
– Strengthen body image
– Reduce self-criticism
– Encourage kindness toward self and others

A Final Encouragement

You might say:

'The more you notice the good in yourself, the better you'll feel – inside and out. The mirror isn't just for checking how we look, it's for reminding us of who we are'.

This is a small but mighty habit that can quietly reshape how your child sees themselves – not just today, but for life.

SELF-HAVENING: A Super-Sized Hug for the Mind

In my earlier book '*First Aid for Your Child's Mind*', I introduced a gentle yet powerful technique called **Havening** – a psycho-sensory approach developed by Dr. Ronald Ruden that helps reduce emotional distress and build resilience.

At its heart, **Havening Techniques** involve applying soothing touch to areas like the arms, hands, and face, often in a hug-like fashion. When we stroke the sides of our arms, just as we might if giving ourselves a reassuring cuddle, the brain begins to release feel-good chemicals such as serotonin and oxytocin – helping the nervous system settle and the mind feel safe.

I've chosen to include it here, at the end of this book, because I believe this technique is something every child and teenager should have in their emotional toolkit. Learning how to comfort yourself – to gently re-centre in times of upset, pressure, or uncertainty – is a vital skill in today's world. And Havening is just that: a way to give yourself the emotional equivalent of a supersized hug, exactly when you need it most.

Before introducing this to your child, I recommend trying it yourself first. Not only will you get a better feel for how the technique works, but you'll also experience first-hand how calming it can be – like a gentle reset for the brain, delivered through the fingertips.

As well as sensory input – in the form of soothing touch – you'll also be encouraging your child to picture themselves doing simple, calming movements.

In the first example, I suggest imagining yourself *walking barefoot on a sandy beach*.

These visualisations help create a sense of ease and comfort. You can tailor the examples to suit your child's interests, but here are a few to get started:

- Pedalling along on their bicycle
- Stirring cake mixture in a bowl with a wooden spoon
- Brushing their hair with a large hairbrush
- Walking through the woods
- Swimming backstroke in a pool
- Jumping on a trampoline

Follow these instructions:

- While seated, cross your arms in an X across your chest and place your hands on your shoulders.
- Gently begin to stroke down the sides of your upper arms to your elbows, with the palm of your hands.
- Each time your hands reach the elbows, lift them up to the shoulders once more.
- And repeat. Keep the motion light, slow and rhythmic.
- Continue to do this and close your eyes.
- Now imagine you're *walking barefoot along a warm, sandy beach*. With each step that you take in the sand, count aloud from the number one to twenty.
- Open your eyes and relax your arms.
- Keeping your head still, gently move your eyes to the right, then to the left. Back to the right, and again to the left.

- Repeat this slow, side-to-side eye movement about ten times.
- Close your eyes and begin to stroke the sides of the upper arms once more and now imagine yourself *jumping on a trampoline*. Each time you bounce up in the air, count aloud again from one to twenty.
- Open your eyes and relax your arms.
- Now take your hands and gently stroke your face – across the forehead, down the cheeks, around the mouth and repeat three times.
- Close your eyes again, cross your arms in an X and again, from the shoulders begin to stroke the sides of your arms.
- Imagine yourself *skipping through a meadow on a sunny day* and with each step you take, count aloud from one to twenty.
- Open your eyes and stop stroking your arms.

What you've just done is create a cascade of calming brainwaves – helping your system release feel-good chemicals like serotonin. You may already notice a shift in how you feel. If the uncomfortable feelings are still lingering, it's perfectly fine to repeat the process.

Getting into a regular routine of using this Havening process – say, each morning before school and every evening before bedtime, will have a cumulative effect. Your child's sense of wellbeing will begin to improve naturally, simply and easily.

IN THE THERAPY ROOM

When the voices never stop

When I first met Rishi, aged 15, he was struggling with the emotional fallout of a few cruel comments made about his body online. The posts hadn't gone viral. They weren't from strangers. But they stung. And like many teenagers, Rishi's mind had quickly magnified them – from 'a few mean words' into an all-encompassing belief that 'everyone' thought he looked wrong – overweight, too short, no 6-pack.

In our sessions, it became clear that this wasn't just about a handful of comments made on one occasion – he was worried that he'd become a bit of a joke amongst all his classmates and so he felt more exposed. Those few unkind words had seeped into his sense of self. 'It's like they're in my school bag… in my phone… even in my bedroom at home', he told me, describing how that one particular classmate's voice seemed to follow him everywhere.

The first step was to quieten down those internal echoes. I gently challenged the sweeping generalisations, replacing 'everyone thinks there's something wrong with me' with more balanced perspectives. His parents supported this at home by introducing a daily ritual of positive reflection – a journal of small wins and moments of joy, helping his brain to rebalance its' focus.

Next, we explored ways to reconnect Rishi with his body – not through sport (which he disliked), but through movement that felt good: trampolining, walking the dog, or just dancing in his bedroom. The goal wasn't to fix his body. It was to help him feel at home in it again.

We also worked with visualisation. I guided him through a gentle hypnosis exercise, where he imagined sitting beneath his favourite oak tree, surrounded by the people (and pets!) who loved him most. In turn, I had each one give him a message of kindness and reassurance.

We then 'rewrote' the screen of his phone, replacing cruel words with these imagined affirmations – because the pictures we hold in our minds shape how we feel in our bodies. By creating this internal circle of safety, Rishi began to rebuild his confidence. The comments still hurt, but they no longer defined him.

Keep This in Mind

If there's one message to carry with you from this chapter, it's that body image isn't fixed – it's shaped. Shaped by our words, our actions, and the quiet, everyday choices we make.

Your child doesn't need perfection; they need perspective. A steady hand, a calm voice, and the reassurance that they are more than how they look. With your support, and a few tools like Havening in their back pocket, they can begin to build the kind of self-image that lasts – grounded in kindness, not comparison. And that really is something worth growing into.

FINAL THOUGHTS

I hope this book has given you something more than information – I hope it's offered encouragement, clarity, and a quiet confidence that small changes truly can make a difference. Because they do.

Helping children develop a healthier relationship with food isn't about perfection. It's about noticing patterns, shifting habits, and creating a home where mealtimes feel safe and positive. Whether your child is fussy, anxious, overindulging, concerned about their size and shape, you now have a toolkit to guide them – one meal, one moment at a time.

You don't have to do everything at once. In fact, the most lasting changes often begin slowly – with one phrase, one routine, one conversation that lands just right.

Remember to revisit your Wish List – writing down all the changes and new habits you think your family would benefit from. And then, reduce that number down into a manageable few things you'll focus on first.

Remember too, to plan ahead and get some dates in the diary for your Family Meetings. Working collaboratively will not only lighten your workload but make success more likely.

Thank you for taking the time to read, to reflect, and to lead your family forward. However far you've come already, or however much lies ahead, please know this:

- your efforts matter
- your words matter
- and you're doing better than you think.

Let this be the beginning of a calmer, kinder journey – for you, and for your child.

I wish you and your family a happy, healthy future.

Alicia

**For more information,
visit my website www.aliciaeaton.co.uk**

Citations for Research Studies and Statistics

1. **ARFID in DSM-5 and Diagnosis Rates**
- American Psychiatric Association. (2013). *Diagnostic and Statistical Manual of Mental Disorders* (5th ed.). Arlington, VA: American Psychiatric Publishing.
- Beat Eating Disorders. (2023). 'ARFID diagnoses up fivefold in UK children.' https://www.beateatingdisorders.org.uk

2. **Parental Underestimation of Child's Weight**
- Lundahl, A., Kidwell, K. M., & Nelson, T. D. (2014). Parental underestimates of child weight: a meta-analysis. *International Journal of Obesity*, 38(5), 651–658. https://doi.org/10.1038/ijo.2013.130:contentReference{index=}

3. **Childhood Obesity Rates in France, UK, and US**
- World Health Organization (2024). *Childhood Obesity Surveillance Initiative*.
- NHS Digital. (2023). *National Child Measurement Programme, England 2022/23 School Year*.
- Centers for Disease Control and Prevention (CDC). (2023). *Prevalence of Childhood Obesity in the United States*. https://www.cdc.gov/obesity/data/childhood.html

4. **Yale Food Addiction Scale for Children**
- Schiestl, E. T., Gearhardt, A. N., et al. (2023). Development and validation of the Child Yale Food Addiction Scale 2.0. *Appetite*, 184, 106464. https://doi.org/10.1016/j.appet.2023.106464:contentReference{index=3}

5. **Global Study on Food Addiction in Children**
- Gearhardt, A. N., & Schulte, E. M. (2023). Prevalence and correlates of food addiction symptoms in youth: A global review. *Journal of Behavioral Addictions*, 12(1), 34–50. https://doi.org/10.1556/2006.2023.00010:contentReference{index=4}

6. **Adolescent Obesity Projections and Ultra-Processed Food Impact**
- Baird, S., Choonara, S., Azzopardi, P. S., et al. (2025). A call to action: a second Lancet Commission on adolescent health and wellbeing. *The Lancet*, 405(10398), 1871–1932. https://doi.org/10.1016/S0140-6736(25)00503-3

7. **Early Childhood Weight and Long-Term Obesity Risk**
- van Grieken, A., et al. (2025, May). *Tracking childhood overweight: Risk patterns from early years to adolescence in the Generation R Study*. Presented at the European Congress on Obesity, Málaga, Spain. Summary via The Guardian: https://www.theguardian.com/society/2025/may/11/being-overweight-as-a-young-child-could-double-risk-of-adult-obesity-research-shows

8. **American Academy of Sleep Medicine Guidelines**
- Paruthi, S., Brooks, L. J., D'Ambrosio, C., et al. (2016). Consensus statement: Recommended amount of sleep for paediatric populations. *Journal of Clinical Sleep Medicine*, 12(6), 785–786. https://doi.org/10.5664/jcsm.5866 (Mentioned but not fully cited in manuscript)

9. **Hypermobility and Eating Sensitivities**
- Castori, M., et al. (2017). Ehlers–Danlos syndrome hypermobility type and gastrointestinal involvement: A review. *Digestive and Liver Disease*, 49(7), 636–642. https://doi.org/10.1016/j.dld.2017.03.025:contentReference{index=5}

10. **Biology of Belief – Bruce Lipton**
- Lipton, B. H. (2005). *The Biology of Belief: Unleashing the Power of Consciousness, Matter & Miracles*. Mountain of Love/Elite Books.

ABOUT ALICIA EATON

Alicia Eaton is an experienced therapist, speaker, and author who has spent over two decades helping families create healthier habits – not just around food, but in all areas of life. Originally trained as a Montessori teacher who ran her own school for five years, she went on to study Developmental Psychology at the Anna Freud Centre in London, as well as working in their parent/toddler support groups. Here she deepened her understanding of how children learn, behave and grow, as well as the many challenges that parents face.

Alicia's clinical background includes training as an Integrative Psychotherapist and Clinical Hypnotherapist, alongside advanced training in NLP (Neuro-Linguistic Programming) with world-renowned hypnotist Paul McKenna. Further specialist trainings include Teaching Mindfulness at Oxford University's Mindfulness Centre and Childhood Obesity at the National Centre for Eating Disorders.

For over 20 years, she has run a successful practice on Harley Street in London, specialising in changing habits, behaviours, and emotional responses in both children and adults.

She is also a bestselling author whose books include *Stop Bedwetting in 7 Days*, (recommended by NHS Clinics in the UK and by doctors and paediatricians around the world); *Words That Work: How to Get*

Kids to Do Almost Anything, and *First Aid for Your Child's Mind* – now also published in Germany, Hungary, Romania, Greece, UAE, Vietnam and China.

She has twice been voted a winner in the Global Health & Pharma Mental Health Awards, including 'Most Innovative Practitioner'. With a practical, compassionate approach, Alicia continues to help families navigate the challenges of modern life, helping them to raise confident, emotionally resilient children, using her unique blend of psychology and practical parenting advice.

Visit website for more details: www.aliciaeaton.co.uk